The Success Mindset

Take back the leadership of your mind

Paola Knecht

Publisher: Knecht Publishing

ISBN: 978-3-033-08772-9

Cover Illustration: David Colon

Cover Design: David Colon

Editor: Kirsten Rees | Book Editor & Author Coach

Disclaimer

This book details the author's personal experiences and opinions about mental and physical health. The author and this book are not a replacement for your healthcare provider.

The author and publisher are providing this book and its contents on an "as is" basis and make no representations or warranties of any kind with respect to this book or its contents.

You understand that this book is not intended as a substitute for consultation with a licensed healthcare practitioner, such as your physician. Before you begin any healthcare programme, or change your lifestyle in any way, you should consult your physician or another licensed healthcare practitioner to ensure that you are in good health and that the examples contained in this book will not harm you.

This book provides content related to physical and/or mental health issues. As such, use of this book implies your acceptance of this disclaimer.

Unless otherwise indicated, all the client names and identifying traits have been changed to protect the privacy of individuals.

Connect with the author:

Instagram: @paolaknecht_author

Twitter: @PaolaKnecht

Website: www.my-mindpower.com

Email: paola.knecht@my-mindpower.com

Contents

Dedication

To my mother, who is my life force inspiration.

To my father, who guides me from heaven and always believed in me.

What is your idea of success?

*Y*ou have the power to define your own success. Everything you need to know about how to live an abundant and wonderful life on your own terms, already sits within you. All you have to do is to look inside, and take back what truly belongs to you. In this book, we will embark together on a journey that will reveal what it really takes to live a life with true meaning.

Success today is deeply shaped by what political leaders, Hollywood stars, influencers, business gurus, and societal institutions tell us success should look like. But the definition of your own success should be something very personal, right? You have the power to design your own success or at least you will after reading this book.

The endless race of reaching 'success' on the collective societal terms seems to throw us on a never-ending spiral of wishes and desires in the outward, competitive world. Study, get a job, form a family, earn enough for financial stability or freedom, and remain a consumer of all the latest technological gadgets, cars, clothing, food, entertainment, health, and so on.

We follow, some happily and some others reluctantly, because we think we have no choice. If the political, business, and cultural leaders are telling me 'this is success', and that's how we should shape the societal structure of the world, then who am I to question it?

I propose that we take back the leadership of our own minds. To start consciously designing our own meaning of success. All the truly great leaders and creators of ancient and modern times transcended in time and space with their contributions. They found the real meaning for their life and designed their success around their personal meaning.

In my journey as a professional coach, I have met many people who aspired and eventually got to live the 'success-like' common life. They have a stable job, financial stability, a nice house, a loving family to look after. Almost as if they have achieved the collective definition of success. Nevertheless, they come to me for counselling, claiming to feel stuck.

A client of mine, a successful businesswoman working for a big pharmaceutical company in a position of power, came to see me one day telling me that she felt in distress. *"I have everything I have wished for; I thought that I loved my job, my husband, and the privileged life we have built together; but one day, I woke up in the morning and I felt empty. I feel as if half of my life is already gone and that I have missed something very important, but I'm not really sure what it is."*

This is not an uncommon statement; in fact, most of the people who come to my practice seem to experience the same sort of feeling.

Suddenly, they wake up one day and realise there is little meaning in what they have in their life. Job has become boring and dreadful; house feels like a prison; quality family time is lacking. They also realise that money cannot buy health. Some call it the 'mid-life crisis'; I prefer to call it the 'confrontation to reality' crisis. It's the moment you feel you wake up from a dream, and realise that half of your life already passed by but you don't know who you are yet. You feel that life is lacking passion and meaning.

What went wrong? Why is normality not enough anymore?

As a lifelong student of the concept of leadership and success, and by intensely researching the traits of great leaders and linking this knowledge with my experience as a professional coach, I have realised that even if those great leaders and creators had very different paths in life, there are some fundamental truths about their mindset that you can identify the moment you start observing the dominant traits in them. Regardless of what activity they do, these blueprints follow the same pattern.

My purpose with this book is to help you regain the leadership of your own mind by sharing with you those patterns, what I have called the eleven pillars. These pillars are by no means an exhaustive list; however, after a lifelong research and study, and following the stories and different paths of great leaders, I found that those eleven traits or 'pillars' that I reveal in this book were present in all of them.

They are certainly the most predominant ones that have helped great leaders and successful people from all paths of life to master the journey of self-discovery. My aim is to expose them to you in a way that serves you as a guideline and at the same time gives you enough room for reflection in finding your own path. At the end of each pillar, I include actions or exercises for reflection that will help you reinforce your learning and understanding from each of them.

What differentiates the ordinary person from the extraordinary one? That is the central question that we will unwrap together. My personal wish is that you dare to live an extraordinary life, a life that is in tune with your own personal definition of success and thus gives you real joy and meaning. I want to help you by giving you the tools and insights that others followed too and made it happen for them.

Many of us feel trapped. Rushing through the years to have a life we didn't consciously design by ourselves. We have been following a path to a 'success story' that maybe was not our real story.

If you resonate with this feeling, you might be wondering: What can I do to rewrite my story and become my own version of success?

With this book, I want to make you a proposition: start to look for success inwards. Join those who silently build human societies that are less focused on targeted external success. Rather, define success as coming back to the joy of being who you want to be, and doing what you want to do.

Are you ready to discover more about your extraordinary self?

Come with me, let's do it together!

First Pillar

Discover your vision

" *All* men dream, but not equally. Those who dream by the night in the dusty recesses of their mind waken the day to find that it was vanity; but the dreamers of the day are dangerous, for they may act their dreams with open eyes, to make it possible."

- T. E. Lawrence

You have a vision, even if you don't know about it yet.

When I was a little girl, I used to go to my balcony nearly every night to do some stargazing. I looked for the brightest star that was visible during the summer nights. I believed there was a fantastic world that existed in that remote bright star.

Through the years, I learned that the brightest star visible in the sky above Northern Mexico, is called the Polaris, commonly known as the North Star. It is the brightest in the constellation of the Urse Minor, located in the northern celestial pole. Every time I looked at this star, I felt like, if there is ever the possibility for interstellar travel, this is the destination I should aim to go for.

Back then, I did not really know what it meant to have a destination, or a path to follow. I just knew that I liked how bright this star was shining in the sky, and I wanted to be part of it; I felt that I was being part of something mysterious, beyond my comprehension; that fascinated me and made me curious about discovering this beautiful mystery we call life.

To have *a vision*, is to believe that we are meant for something bigger than we can see. To find the meaning of our life beyond the inevitable cycle of birth and death. We don't want to feel alone and insignificant. We want to feel we belong somewhere, that our lives are meaningful to someone, or we are destined for something great. It is that longing for something bigger than our own life, what keeps us alive. Aiming every day to find what it is and what is our pathway to meet our destiny.

If you don't know what you want or where you are going, how can you be certain you are living your best life?

I have asked myself this last question since a very early age. The first time this question came so clear to me, I was around eight years old, with my mother driving home after school. Sitting in the passenger side, I observed the dense traffic; the rows of cars, one after the other, some racing to escape the line. Watching the faces and expressions of the people, some looked angry and anxious; others seemed to enjoy the slow pace. I heard the torrent of honking noises.

I started to wonder: *Where are all these people going?* My mother, as if she could read my thoughts, made an interesting comment, "You know, Paola? Sometimes when I see all these people, all of them driving in all different directions, I wonder, where the hell they are going that they always drive in such a hurry?"

All of us are going *somewhere*. I thought that innocent question back then with no real intention, but some curiosity stayed with me for sure, because I became obsessed with that question myself for many years after. *Where am I going? Do all people know where they are going? Is it important that we know?*

Definitely, to look for the answer to that question is what a true meaningful life is all about.

I found myself looking after and admiring people who could answer that question for themselves. I remember watching musicians, writers, athletes and businesspeople that looked very happy and satisfied with their life, and I wondered if they always knew what they wanted to do with their lives or if it was just a coincidence that they became happy and successful. *Can you design your own life and your own success or is it a matter of luck and chance?*

As my appetite for finding the answer grew, I decided to look for evidence by reading and studying the biographies of extraordinary people I admired. They reached something they desired which seemed impossible, and left a legacy behind.

I realised indeed, I was not the only one in the search for this quest and that it is as common as the sunset. Most of the ancient and contemporary world thinkers actually began with such questions as a central quest to understand their human existence.

I also found out that regular people don't ask such questions for themselves. After the golden childhood years, most people live their life in a hurry, trying to chase something, but without a clear understanding or direction. They mainly react to the circumstances of the environment. There is no internal drive; but rather an external pull.

When I put that question to people in my role as a coach, many do not have clarity on where they are going or how they want their lives to be. During our sessions, when I asked simple questions like, 'How satisfied are you with your life?', most of them answered that life was 'okay', or 'it could be worse'. When I asked: "What makes you wake up in the morning?" The most shocking answer I have heard so far has been: "I don't know!"

With time, it has become clearer to me: The difference between regular and extraordinary people is that the latter recognised what is moving them. In other words, they have a vision of what they want to achieve in their lives. They know what to work and live for. People with a successful mindset not only think about what they want to get in terms of material things, but more about how their vision can help others and how the world would become a better place if they could fulfil that vision.

One of the personalities I admire the most is Nelson Mandela. He had a very clear vision that dictated every action and decision he took in his life. In his book, *Long Walk to Freedom*, translated into English it says, "I have dedicated my whole life to fight for the African people. I have fighted against the white domination and also against the black domination. I have caressed the skin of a democratic and free society, where everybody would live in harmony, with equal opportunities. It is a dream for which I aspire to live and which I aspire to reach, but if it's necessary, it is a dream for which I am willing to die for".

His vision guided his existence, in all his conscious and unconscious actions. Ultimately, reaching a position where he could influence the destiny of his country and move towards reaching his vision: becoming the first black president in South Africa.

The vision is the dream, that thing you really want to reach; this person you want to become.

It is often said, 'Small men have small dreams, big men have big dreams'. It is not the accumulation of power and wealth that make people big, but their desire of driving positive change in societies. Big dreams require courage and action. Nevertheless, a path worthwhile taking may not necessarily be easy, but it will certainly be meaningful and will take you closer to where you want to go. Like Norman Vincent Peale said, "Shoot to the moon, even if you miss you will land among the stars".

A vision has a very powerful effect in the way you live your life. Most people feel that their faith depends on external things that happen around them. Since we are young, our parents, our school, and societies show us how we should behave, what we should believe, and what success means. We develop an external sense of who we are, and what we are supposed to do, based on the opinions of others. We end up developing a sort of personality that fits mainly with the external expectations, but does not necessarily reflect what we really want or who we really are.

So, go ahead and find out your vision!

I can hear your next question. *Alright, I get it but, what if I don't know how to find my vision?*

I will show you how shortly. But first, give it a try!

ACTION:

Get a piece of paper and pen. Reflect for a moment about your life. Where are you going? Where would you like to see yourself in ten years from now? How about in thirty years from now?

Take a photo of your notes and share them with me on Instagram by using the hashtag #SuccessWithKnecht

How to identify and connect with your vision

*S*tarting the exciting journey of finding your vision in life is easier than you think. While it does take a lot of self-observation, I will show you how to carve out the time in your busy schedule and guide you with a methodical approach. Let me guide you through this simple but powerful method.

The very first step is to identify the activities you love to do. It helps to make a small retrospection and recall all the things and dreams you had as a child. Did you dream of being a ballet dancer? A teacher? An artist? What did you dream about? Did you love to paint or draw? All those memories give you a good hint of the activities or topics that you inherently love. They do not come from the external influences you have received as you grew up, but more from that internal compass - your heart - which never lies.

"If you don't love something, you're not going to go the extra mile, work the extra weekend, challenge the status quo as much."

- Steve Jobs

Once you have identified the topics and activities you love, the next thing to identify is the activities you are good at. Are you good with numbers? Cooking? Talking to people? Organising events? You can ask people close to you: your parents, colleagues, and closest friends might see qualities in you that you have not seen yourself.

The intersection between what you love and what you are good at will help you to identify what your *passion is*. As the typical dictionary definition describes it, passion is "the intense desire or enthusiasm for something". You will know what your passion is when you realise that doing a certain activity or learning about a certain topic brings you a lot of joy. The time you spend doing it vanishes; you can do this activity for hours and hours and you never grow tired of it.

First identify your passion, now think about how you can connect your passion with activities you can get paid for. When you connect the things you love with the activities you can get paid for, you discover your *vocation,* which basically means that you put your passion at the service of others.

ACTION:

To find your vocation you can ask yourself simple questions.

What are the activities that I currently do, enjoy, and I get compensated for?

What types of activities bring me the most rewards?

Make a list of the top ten things you believe you are very good at.

Once you have more clarity about your vocation, then you are ready to start exploring a bit further, so you can ask yourself the following: What can I do to contribute in a positive way to the world? Which aspects of my work can I further improve and develop so that I can bring a positive impact to the life of others?

The answer to those questions will bring you to discover…

…your mission.

To find your mission, you can ask yourself simply: Why I am here? What is the contribution I want to make in this world?

Most of the greatest leaders and successful people of our times have identified their personal mission and they dedicate their lives living for it. For example, Oprah Winfrey, declared that her personal mission is "To be a teacher. And to be known for inspiring my students to be more than they thought they could be".

Vandana Shiva, one of the world's most prominent scientists and environmental activist, found her mission in life when she understood that the biodiversity, food security, and the ancient agricultural practices of many provinces in her native India were in danger of being destroyed. She decided to dedicate her life and scientific work in defence of keeping rural agricultural practices, the protection of the forests, and honouring the women's role in agriculture.

A mission, as you could read in the examples above, is basically an image of how you see and think about the future, and it involves all aspects of your life: How do you see your family? What does your work look like? Where are you living? What are you doing?

To help articulate your mission, write it down. Written words have a very powerful effect on your subconscious mind. Write your mission everywhere where you can see it: in your agenda, as a post-it in a visible place in your office, on a sheet of paper that you can keep in your purse/wallet. Your mission should be present with you every day and it will consciously and unconsciously dictate all your activities.

To have a mission in life is something wonderful because it basically serves as an internal guidance that will define how you will live your life in order to fulfil those goals you have set for yourself. If you have reached this point, congratulations, it's a fantastic achievement of self-discovery!

But it doesn't have to end there: If you want to go a step further, and you dream about making an ever-lasting contribution to the world, something that goes far beyond yourself and your area of influence, then you are approaching the highest and most noble aspiration of human nature: to have a vision.

The bigger the vision and the more unattainable it seems to be, the more it tends to develop into an enduring passion, that could even leave a legacy after you leave this world.

#TheKnechtWay to find your vision

What I love to do + What I am good at + What can I do and get paid for + What I can do to contribute to the world by serving others + How do I see the world as a result of my mission = Vision

Your personal vision will be at the heart and centre of the intersection of your passion, your mission, and your vocation.

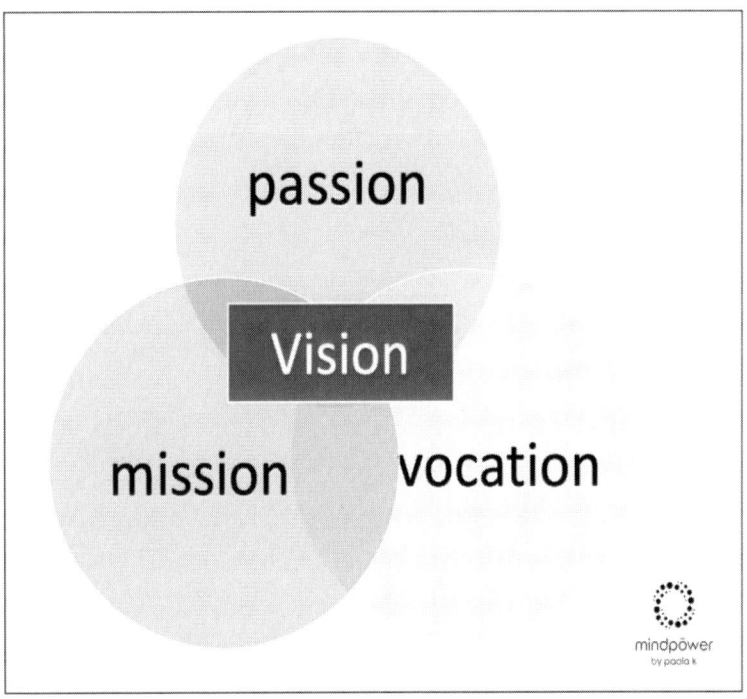

Figure 1: Discover your vision (a.k.a. north star)

The vision should act as your north star: it shows you the ultimate destination, guiding you on your journey to success. It does not tell you specifically how you will get there; but simply acts like a compass. The path is not important at this point. Many people get frustrated because they know where they would like to go but have no clue how to get there. At this point in your journey of self-discovery, the *how* does not really matter. The how will unfold and clear the path as soon as you put your feet into action. What is crucial is to understand where you are going. Where are you investing all your time and energy?

Sound complicated? Let's use a real example. Below, you will find some exercises that will help you go through your own journey of finding your vision using this approach. I have used my own experience of how I found my vision using all the steps.

ACTION:

Following the steps below should guide you well enough in starting to find your vision.

Step 1: Find out what you love

All I did is to schedule some me-time during the day and think about all the things that I really love doing. How do I know what I love to do? I just observed any of my ordinary days and detected which activities, places, or topics I ended up spending most of the time, doing, hearing, seeing, and imagining.

So, after reviewing my daily activities carefully, I found:

1. I love to write
2. I love to read books
3. I love helping people improve their lives through advice and asking questions
4. I love success stories and analyse biographies of extraordinary leaders
5. I love to travel, discovering new cultures and ways of doing things
6. I love walks in nature
7. I love to be with my family and closest friends
8. I love the intersection with arts, literature, science, spirituality, and human nature

Step 2: Things you are very good at:

For this step, I also asked the advice from people that know me well. My family, my colleagues, former mentors and managers, and also my friends. Then I cross-checked with my own perception of what I consider I am best at. After inquiring about it, I realised that:

1. I'm very good at listening and paying attention to people's feelings
2. I'm great at using my intuition to make decisions
3. I'm very good at getting things done
4. I create positive and harmonious relationships with people
5. I'm a good strategist
6. I'm very good with discipline
7. I'm confident in expressing things written and orally
8. I'm good at coping well with uncertainty

Step 3: Discover your passion

After analysing what I love with what I am good at, I connected the dots to find out what I am really passionate about. It turns out, that:

1. I'm passionate about reading and writing topics related to success, leadership, personal development, spirituality, and human nature
2. I'm passionate about helping people improve their lives using everything I have experienced and learned in human nature, science, and business
3. I'm passionate about discovering new places, cultures, and people and I'm a lifelong learner

Step 4: Discover your vocation

To bring my passion to life, it was also necessary to understand what kind of jobs I have been doing and getting paid for, and find out what of those things I really enjoy doing.

In my personal example, I found out that I have been mostly paid for:

- Designing, planning, and executing projects in diverse industries

- Being able to work with people from different countries in different languages and contexts
- Inspiring people and teams to work together and reach great results
- My knowledge in diverse topics related to business, coaching and leadership, accumulated over the last fifteen years

Now, I am a step closer to defining my vocation. A vocation is that magic formula where you combine all the work done above with your passion. So, you combine what you are good at (your gifts and talents) and what you love then bring all this into a job, something you can get paid for.

You can also see it as finding your ideal or dream job: Use your talents and capabilities and allow them to serve what you are passionate about.

In my example, I found out that my vocation can be:

- Becoming a leadership and transformational coach to help people and organisations develop a more positive working environment which unlocks people's full potential
- Becoming a subject matter expert, write and teach about how to connect new lines of knowledge in relation to leadership, human nature, spirituality, and business.

Having a vocation doesn't necessarily mean that you will be strictly rewarded in money for it. For example, if you find out that your true vocation is raising your children and managing a household. Or perhaps you are an advocate of human rights and like to organise voluntary work. In these cases, the form of payment goes beyond thinking about a physical currency. What matters is to connect with what you love and what you are good at with an activity that will contribute to your wellbeing and ultimately, to the world. That is how the real wealth is created. The sky is not actually the limit, you can see and go far beyond!

Step 5. Formulate your mission

My mission had to involve three things: my love for helping people improve their lives; leadership; the active role in contributing in actions towards unity and love in our society; and my skills with writing, organising and creating. My mission statement ended up like this:

"My mission is to help people rediscover themselves and support them in their journey of transformation. As a coach, writer, scientist and life learner, I want to discover new paths of knowledge that will bring us forward as a human race, working in the intersection between science, humanity and spirituality."

Step 6: Putting all the ingredients together: write down your vision.

By now, you may be thinking that this seems like hard work. To arrive at the farthest destination - your vision - required quite some introspection. The good news is that if you really spend the time investing in yourself and getting clarity on this, once you are on the journey of finding your vision, you cannot go back to who you once were. You will want to keep going, to keep discovering how far you can go and who you can become. I believe that spending time in finding your mission and ultimately your vision is the way to go for every person who wants to live a successful and fulfiling life. Because, as Socrates rightly said: "The unexamined life is not worth living".

Back to my example, to formulate my vision I put together all the previous steps into one small, straightforward single statement, which is the equivalent of my north star: my vision. Or also, as I call it, the reason of my life.

"To honour life by living it in the most joyful and supreme way by learning, growing, and sharing. I build projects that transform lives, acting as a bridge between the material and spiritual worlds where love, unity, beauty, and truth are the highest of aims."

Paola Knecht

*A*s you can see, the vision is really aiming for final destination. In my particular example, I do not stop with my mission and passion; rather I go further beyond. You might ask why I did not include in my vision detailed information like my love for writing, etc.

The answer is that I believe a vision should be a statement that goes beyond the how's to get there. Life changes, the world changes and what you loved to do five years ago might not be the same twenty years from now. The vision is something that remains as the 'ultimate goal' so no matter what you do or how you do it, ultimately you want to get there.

I have done the same exercises with some of my clients who wanted to find their vision in life. I recall the case of Lisa, a young MBA graduate. She came to coaching because she wanted to find out what kind of profession she would like to pursue after she finished her MBA. She studied to become a chemist, but during her studies she found out that chemistry was not her real passion. Then she decided to do a master's degree in Business Administration so she could be more flexible in getting jobs. As it turned out, she ended up joining big companies and did different sorts of corporate jobs. At one point, one morning while getting prepared for work, she looked at herself in the mirror and said, "This is not me".

We worked together on the six step-guide described above so we could dig into the things that are most important for her in life and find the way to link her talents and interests with a bigger cause where she could find a more profound meaning about who she is and the things she does. Her vision, a short single statement, ended up being quite surprising. She allowed me to share it with you.

Lisa's vision is to "Contribute to people's happiness and well beings by developing new fragrances and sensations". She created handmade soaps and creams that she could produce at home and ended up opening her own online shop! With the knowledge gained in her chemistry studies, and her passion for flower gardening she found an interesting link between what she was good at with what she was passionate about and this awareness helped her to understand her vocation and ultimately her vision.

To find out your vision on a higher level, it is necessary to understand what really makes you happy and ask yourself, "How can I live a more joyful life, and how can I be the best person I can possibly be?" And to answer those questions, it is necessary to do all the previous inner work.

The vision should represent the highest goal; it should certainly be bold, even if it looks unattainable, as it is the path of excellence and self-discovery. It's a never-ending learning process. Tatiana Clouthier, current Mexican Secretary of Economy, started her professional career as an English and history teacher. Her love for Mexico and her desire to change the controversial political landscape of the country and to contribute to the transformation of it, motivated her to get involved in different political roles in the state of Nuevo Leon until she got one of the first line roles of the government today. Thanks to her charisma, competence and popularity, many people see her as a potential running candidate for the next presidential elections in 2024!

This is the power of having a bold vision. It will guide consciously and unconsciously all your actions. You will find yourself waking up every morning for something that means a lot for you: for the bright future it represents. No one finds inspiration in waking up without knowing where life is leading you. No one can be truly happy thinking that the past was better, or without knowing what to live for. Having a vision will definitely set you on the right path: you will wake up every morning looking positively towards the future, and you will give everything you've got.

Dare greatly

Andrea, a middle-aged woman, an executive assistant and a mother of two toddlers, came to see me for coaching advice. When we sat together and started our conversation over a cup of coffee, she explained to me about her troubles in getting things done in her life. "My biggest frustration is that nobody helps me, not even in the basic duties of the household. I have to do everything by myself. I am the only one who worries about all my kids' whereabouts. My husband helps me but is not enough. At work, it is the same. It seems like nobody can do a good job. I have to correct all the things that my colleagues do wrong without any recognition. I am simply tired".

An expression of frustration and anger was evident on her face. I listened to the rest of the long list of complaints she had about every aspect of her life. At one point during the conversation, I paused her and asked: "Andrea, it seems like you have been through a lot and you struggle to find pleasure in your daily life. I wonder, what is really going on here?"

She looked at me puzzled. "What do you mean?" she said.

"What is really important for you? What motivates you to wake up every morning?" I asked.

"Hmm. Interesting question. The thing is, I don't really know what I'm doing. All I know is that I wake up every morning in a hurry, already thinking of all I have to do during the day. I wish I could have some time to stop and think more about myself".

"Imagine you make time for yourself to reflect on this. What is the first thing you see?"

Andrea closed her eyes for a moment and kept silent for a couple of minutes. Then she replied: "That's my problem. I don't see anything. Nothing that I do now really moves me. My kids make me happy when they are not driving me crazy I guess that's it. I cannot say it is my job. I like what I do, but I do it mostly to pay the bills. I wouldn't do it for free. I guess, I'm afraid to confront myself".

"Confront yourself. Tell me more about it."

"Ahh ... hmm, well. I guess it's just, you know, I am afraid to find out that all I do has no meaning for anybody. That nobody cares about me. And so, I often think that is a waste of time to think about all this and then I just move on with whatever I'm doing in the moment".

"Andrea, what is really meaningful for you?" I insisted.

After a long pause in silence, she said: "I want to have time for myself. I want to have time to paint. You know, I used to paint canvas in acrylic. I had a very good eye to capture the essence of landscapes and express it in my painting".

"Wonderful. What stops you from continuing painting?" I wondered.

"Hmm. Good question. I just thought I don't have the time anymore. You know, my work, my kids, all the household activities I never thought I could make space for that. But I miss it ... I guess I should try to make some time to come back to that".

During our following coaching conversations, we worked on a plan to help Andrea to become more efficient on her daily activities but also making sure she kept a space for herself so she can do things that are meaningful for her, and deep dived into the six steps of finding her vision. After two months, she came back to share with me some news:

"Guess what, Paola? I'm doing it. I'm going to quit my job and I will open a workshop for kids to teach them different painting techniques. You cannot imagine how happy I feel to do this step. I will be able to spend most of my working time doing what I was really meant to do: painting. And I will share my knowledge with others! Finally, I have found my personal vision: To express the beauty of life through painting and teaching others to find their own expression too!"

Like Andrea, many people feel stuck at one point in their lives because they are afraid to confront their consciousness when it tells them that the direction their life is taking (if there is a direction at all) is not the path that will take them to their personal realisation. The awareness of this can come in many different ways, for example when you feel frustration with little things, when you find your capacity of being patient decreases; when you abuse in specific behaviours like overconsumption of alcohol, excessive time on social media, overspending, accumulation of things, etc.

What does it take to finally listen over our consciousness and take righteous action towards what we really want? We will discuss it in more detail throughout the book, but in essence, you have to *dare greatly*. You need to believe that what is in your heart and you hold dear is precisely what you are meant to do. And don't be afraid of how it all unfolds. Trust that your heart, our connection with the divine, is guiding you and having your back.

Sadhguru, a famous mystic and guru from India, says: "If you work incessantly and still your goal is not fulfilled, it doesn't mean it is a failure. It just means you had a great vision".

Don't just aspire to live your life just to make a living and survive. Aspire to live it boldly, aspire to make a difference. Don't live someone else's dreams. One of our main problems as we grow up is that we become numb to our own desires, in favour of being nice and sensible to others. Reclaim your true desires back with no fear nor shame.

No matter how old you are or which stage of life you are in, never measure your goals against others. Instead, measure your own feelings, ambitions and goals against yourself. In other words, keep track of who you are vs. who you want to become and keep lifting the bar high! If that means going against well-meaning advice from your family or friends and standing all for yourself on it, so be it.

"Cherish your visions; cherish your ideals; cherish the music that stirs in your heart, the beauty that forms in your mind, the loveliness that drapes your purest thoughts, for out of them will grow all delightful conditions, all heavenly environment; of these, if you but remain true to them, your world will at last be built to desire is to obtain; to aspire is to achieve."

- James Allen

How your intuition can help in finding your vision

We have covered the topic of finding your vision, parting from the perspective that you have a certain level of knowledge about what you love to do, and how to have a good understanding of yourself. But what happens when you don't even have a clue about what you love?

There is certainly a more powerful way to know yourself: intuition

The meaning of intuition has taken several paths; the one we will discuss here is about how your inner voice can reveal the true nature of who you are, which will bring to your awareness what you are naturally meant to do.

One of the biggest mistakes people make when trying to find and follow their intuition is that they put a lot of thinking into it. They even treat it as an item on a checklist: dedicate five minutes a day to find my intuition. Check! The problem with this approach is that intuition by itself does not require *any thinking*. Quite the contrary. For the intuition to flourish you need to stay very alert in the present moment.

Steve Jobs, the founder of Apple, understood the importance of developing his own vision using his intuition. He said, "People in the Indian countryside don't use their intellect like we do, they use their intuition instead, and their intuition is far more developed than in the rest of the world. Intuition is a very powerful thing, more powerful than intellect, in my opinion. That's had a big impact on my work."

To listen to your intuition, all you need to do is to remain quiet. Observe your presence and surrender to the present moment without any particular thought. You may think this sounds challenging, as you cannot 'stop' your mind from thinking. In fact, there is a way, and the best way is to train yourself to enjoy being here and now. As if you are a little kid; looking at everything around you with no judgement and no attachment.

Surrender to what is happening right now. If thoughts come, observe them, how they come and go like an energy torrent. Franz Kafka, the Czech prominent writer, found his inspiration while writing his most famous novella *Metamorphosis* by connecting to the present. "You need not to leave your room. Remain sitting at your table and listen. You need not to even listen, simply wait. You need not just to even wait, just learn to become quiet, and still, and solitary. The world will freely offer itself to you to be unmasked."

When you surrender to your present moment and you are not worried about the time (past and future), you see with more clarity what you have to do and automatically you start to act, one thing at a time. Nature operates this way: it operates intuitively, wonderfully displaying the miracle of life, without any stress or dissatisfaction. The tree does not get worried about being a tree. A dolphin does not question his nature and wonder if what he is doing is right or wrong the dolphin simply is.

ACTION:

Look every day for moments of silence and observation. Become aware of your surroundings. Stay alert of the mental torrent of thought. The moment you start to see yourself as a 'silent witness' of your thoughts, you have indeed raised a certain level of awareness, from which your intuition will flourish. You will know what to do at any time. And never forget: what guides you from the inside is the feeling of joy that emerges when you let go and accept who you are.

#TheKnechtWay of discovering your vision:

- The first pillar of success is to discover your vision (a.k.a.) north star, or the reason of your life
- To get your vision clarified, you can follow a methodical approach. The formula is to discover:
- What I love to do + What I am good at + What I can do and get paid for + What I can do to contribute to the world by serving others + How do I see the world as a result of my mission = Vision
- If you are unsure what you really love to do, use your intuition to find out
- To connect with your intuition, you need to connect fully to the present and act organically in tune with it
- Stay open to change. Embrace new possibilities, but never lose the track of your vision

Exercises for Reflection:

Let's discover your north star! The questions below and exercises will guide you through each of the recommended steps discussed in this section. You can find a template for this exercise in the downloadable workbook on my website which is listed at the end of the book. Don't forget to share your results with me! Take a screenshot or a photo of your vision statement and share it on Instagram. Remember to tag me and using the hashtag #SuccessWithKnecht as I'll be sharing some of them on my story.

Step 1: Discover what your love

1. *Make an exhaustive list of all the things you love to do.*

2. *If you had all the money in the world, what would you be doing right now?*

3. *List at least five activities that you are doing in your daily life that make you very happy.*

Step 2: What are the things you are very good at?

1. *Ask at least five people (family, friends, colleagues) which things they think you are very good at or most talented in.*

2. *In your own opinion, what are the things you are good at?*

3. *Put your memory to work and write down at least five compliments or good feedback you have received about something you have done at work or in daily affairs by other people.*

Step 3: Passion!

1. *List at least three things you love to do and believe you are good at.*

2. *When you were a kid, what did you want to do when you grew up?*

3. *Which jobs would you accept doing without getting paid?*

Step 4: Define your vocation

1. *List all the paid jobs you have had until now.*

2. *Is there any connection between the activities you have been paid for and what you would love to do?*

3. *Write out some ideas about jobs you would really love to do and be rewarded for in terms of money, satisfaction, resources, etc.*

Step 5: Define your mission

1. *What are your unique personal qualities?*

2. *How can you put those personal and unique qualities in service to others?*

3. *What are your innermost desires?*

4. *How do you imagine you can contribute to making this world a better place?*

Step 6: Discover your north star: Your vision

1. *Imagine how the world would be if you achieve your life's mission. How would it look like?*
2. *Imagine you are on your death bed. If you were to be asked, what would be your last wish before you leave this world what would it be?*
3. *For what would you like to be remembered, after your life on this earth comes to an end?*
4. *What is the legacy you would like to leave behind?*

"Don't aspire to live your life just making a living and surviving. Aspire to live it boldly, aspire to make a difference."

Paola Knecht

Second Pillar

Build a supportive environment to reach your vision

"Never change things by fighting existing reality. To change something, build a new model that makes the existing model obsolete."

- R.B. Fuller

*A*fter doing the exercise from the first pillar, you are now equipped with the invaluable discovery about your north star, your vision.

To follow your vision, you will have to make fundamental changes in your life. To be willing to change is a fairly easy decision, but to create real change is not easy and requires a lot of effort. As it turns out, we humans don't cope very well with change.

American author Robert Greene says it rightfully in his book, *The Laws of Human Nature*: "Everyone understands the need of change in the abstract, but on the day to day, people are creatures of habit".

It is easy to declare that a change is needed, and to even plan for it. However, during the execution, we tend to get attached too strongly to our old habits and patterns. This is one of the key challenges you need to overcome, if you are serious about making fundamental changes that are more in line with your vision.

Colin Cook et al. in the book, *The Power of Impossible Thinking*, propose an interesting approach to start making gradual changes in our already old and imposed habits. The premise behind this is that to change only your way of thinking is not enough; you should also think about building in parallel the supporting structures that allow the change to happen. In other words, what they propose is to set up an *infrastructure* around your life, a supporting environment that allows you to perform small changes in your thinking and your habits, in a progressive, but consistent way.

What does it actually mean, to build up an infrastructure or supporting environment? Using the metaphor of envisioning the construction of a big building, the infrastructure on very general terms will be: the piece of land with the right foundation, the construction materials, the architectural plans or the blueprint of the building, and the frame; which is basically holding the structure the building will have. At the end then comes the installation of the final touches: windows, doors, ceilings, etc. As you see, if all those elements are built in together and in harmony, the result will be a beautiful strong building.

Now let's use this metaphor to build the supporting environment to reach your vision.

Building foundation: Identifying your core values

The foundations of a building are normally invisible to us. We see and admire the great construction, but we do not see what is holding it and keeping it upwards. Even if we cannot see it, the foundations are really the groundwork of the building; it's the base from which the whole construction is sustained. When we are doing something during the day, there is a base as well from which we perform our act. What holds our act 'together'? There are some invisible forces which are influencing us from the 'basement' in what we think, say and do. Those invisible forces are called our core value. Core values are the internal principles and convictions that people choose consciously or unconsciously and which dictate their behaviour.

Most people are aware that values exist and reign our human interaction, but not many know that they can choose them and how their choice is affecting their lives. If you relate to this situation, you can start right now by asking yourself the following questions:

What do you value the most in your life?

Are you living your life in line with what you value the most?

If not, what is getting in the way?

Let's say for example, that a woman called Alicia has the dream to contribute to the eradication of poverty in Africa. She identifies herself with the value of 'equality' and she aspires to make a change in the world by supporting non-profit organisations that operate in Africa with small money contributions. That's for sure a nice start. But then in her daily life, she unconsciously supports the unfair trade conditions imposed against Africa and buys potatoes from the Netherlands instead of supporting local African farming. She buys clothes made in China instead of looking for ways to buy from local African designers.

Those actions clearly show a conflict between what she envisions versus what she is actually doing. She might feel that something is missing, or that she is not being fully consequent in her actions but she does not know why. By raising her awareness to observe every single decision she takes, she can quickly find out that she is not acting fully according to her values. That gives her the power to change her behaviour and her reality; or else, she might discover that this value is not representing who she really is. She has now the possibility to choose other values more in line with her being.

As with all important self-introspection work, finding your core values requires serious and honest thought. American psychologist and author, Brené Brown says in her book, *Dare to Lead* that "Living our values means that we do more than profess our values, we practice them. We walk our talk: we are clear about what we believe and hold important, and we take care that our intentions, words, thoughts and behaviors align with those beliefs".

To find out what are your core values, you must do some introspection work and consider what are the things or principles you hold most dearly in your heart. Maybe you discover that you identify yourself with many values, for example: respect, loyalty, efficiency, courage, commitment, passion, etc. However, it is important to think which are the top two or three that really define who you are and what you believe. If you keep a long list of values it will be hard for you to find out your life priorities.

ACTION:

Here is a good exercise that can help you to select and prioritise your values. Find a quiet place and take a blank sheet of paper and a pen with you;

1. List all values you consider to be very important to you; you can find a comprehensive list of values on Appendix I at the end of this book to help you with the journey. Download a free template for this exercise in the downloadable booklet available on the Success Mindset website.

2. Select ten values that describe you at your best.

3. Try to classify your values in bigger categories and consider if another value can comprise the others. For example, if you list as your core values joy, good humour, and positivity, try to test if one contains the other. In this case, for example, joy means staying positive and finding good humour in daily life. Then you could pick joy as the leading value for you.

4. Reduce your list to one or two values. Those have to be the absolute ones that really define who you are. It will be a hard job to do, but remember that the ones you chose can be tested in the others you wanted to choose and most likely you will see that one contains the other in one way or another.

You must stick to one or two values, which are really important for you and really speak for who you are. Jim Collins, in his book, *Good to Great* says, "If you have more than three priorities, you have no priorities". If every value has the same importance for you, then nothing really dictates your life or nothing is really a driver for you. In my personal example, my two core values ended up being authenticity and love. Even if

I had many others that I identified with like health, transcendence, freedom, joy, and unity, I realised that most of those secondary values come from a place of love and authenticity.

Now the next question is, how do we convert our values into our blueprint or set of behaviours?

Once we have our solid base, the next crucial element is to create the blueprint of how it will look; the architectural plan. If we take this analogy back to our vision, what we need to do is to take a look at our behaviours, which are the precursors of our actions.

Our behaviours are the way in which we act towards people and the way we conduct ourselves in daily life. Our behavioural traits are mainly shaped by our values, which influence our thoughts, manifest our emotions, and ultimately translates into our actions in the external environment.

Architects must design the blueprint with the utmost precision; they need to define everything that is relevant so that the building will last. For example, they include the foundation plan, the floor plan, the ceiling and framing, the windows and doors, and interior elevations among other technical specifications. Of course, the idea here is not to give you all the details of a real architectural plan of how to build a building; what I am really after, is to use this as a metaphor to describe how our behaviours are similar to the blueprint of a building: Without understanding the plan, architects cannot build a building; in our case, without understanding our behaviours and where they are taking us in detail, we could never reach our vision or north star.

In the first pillar, you started tracing your life plan by defining your vision. So far in this section you also started defining the foundation (your core values), which will sustain everything you plan to build. Now, it's time to go a step further and get specific about how you can reach your vision while observing and modifying your behaviours.

When you are aware of your behaviours, you will understand how to change and direct them. A good way to start would be to dedicate one or two days to purely observe and register them. You can, for example, start a journal and write all the things you do during the day. Then after you have registered this for a couple of days, review them and ask yourself: *How many of these activities and behaviours helped me to get a step closer to reaching my goals?* If you find out that not many are really helping you, think about what you can modify in your daily routine to get a better alignment with your values and your vision.

The best way to start modifying your behaviour is to start with small changes that will eventually affect your broader perceptions and actions in the bigger picture.

Let's illustrate this last point with an example that I have seen quite often in real life. Let's assume that you found out, that one of your core values is self-respect. In this imaginary scenario, you are working at an insurance company, and you have a very dominant, aggressive boss. For instance, your boss likes to blame and shame people when a mistake happens and threatens to fire everyone if they don't perform as he expects.

You have been working in this company for seven years, and you have had enough of this behaviour and the toxic culture that dominates the office environment. You complain to your colleagues, and they rant about him as well, so you contribute to the office gossip. However, when your boss confronts you directly and blames you for something, you freeze. You do not stand up to him. You timidly leave his office feeling frustrated and angry, return to your desk and keep working. You cannot concentrate anymore, because the image of your boss and the F* word will not leave your head. It's obvious that your frustration is the consequence of not behaving in line with your core value of self-respect.

In this case, which small and progressive changes could you do, to live in tune with the value of self-respect? First of all: Recognise that the source of the problem lies within you. It has been an unconscious decision to accept not to live according to your core value. The moment you become aware of this you have done the first and most important step towards slowly changing and shaping the new set of behaviours.

Once you have recognised and accepted that you have not been behaving in line with your core-value of self-respect, the next step would be to identify how to modify the current behaviour and replace it with a new behaviour more in line with your value. For example, using the scenario above (dealing with a toxic boss), the first thing you could do is stop the complaining and gossiping. You have recognised that it is in you to demand and ask for self-respect and the first rule is to also give respect to others.

This would be a small change, but a good one that will take you to the next step: Prepare to directly confront your boss. The next time you experience a hostile situation with your boss, you can demand better treatment. You can do it with respect, with a firm voice. This step could be scary for the majority of us. For many reasons, we are terrified to confront our bosses or other people of authority when they treat us unfairly. Many of us would be scared to lose the job, or just wouldn't want to start a potential conflict with a 'superior' due to the hierarchical status. But if you chose the value of self-respect at the core of who you are, then it will feel natural to you to act according to this value and demand the respect you deserve. With every incremental step you do, and the bolder the actions you take in every step, the more the fear will eventually go away.

Robert Greene, in his book, *The Laws of Human Nature* defines fearlessness as a muscle that we used to exercise naturally during our childhood; but with the passing years it gets atrophied because we acquire more timidity as we grow older.

Do you remember how you used to ask your parents for everything? If you wanted ice cream, a toy, or to go to the park. You said it boldly, right? If you are a parent of small children, I am sure you can relate. Children do not understand political correctness, civilised consensus, or anything like that. They just ask for what they want. They are congruent and articulated with their wishes. They are hungry, they ask for food. They are bored? They ask for attention. To articulate our wishes with no sense of shame, but of legitimacy, is part of our forgotten nature.

To gain the fearless muscle back, we have to train it again and put it back in a fitness program: You have to start with small exercises like speaking up and expressing your opinion, and progressively taking on greater demands. Once you grow this muscle strong, you will regain the confidence that you can do everything you want in life and demand it with a fearless attitude. We will take a more detailed look at how to overcome the fear of failure when we reach the fifth pillar.

Build the frame: Develop a set of daily habits

We have almost all the set-up of our building. We laid the basic foundation which is the choice of our core values; then we developed the architectural plan, which is the recognition and shape of our behaviours. Now it's time to start building the frame; the pillars that will sustain the construction, according to our architectural plan. What is the key ingredient in building strong pillars of behaviour? What will keep your building safe from falling apart? I suspect you are guessing right your daily habits!

For a new set of behaviours to 'settle in', we must convert and integrate those new behaviours into a set of daily habits. Most neuroscientists, philosophers, and students of human behaviour have agreed with the fact that we humans are animals of habit. We like to have structures in place that help us to deal with the otherwise 'chaotic' world we live in. Structures help us to diminish the feeling of uncertainty and make us feel like we are in a safe place; Habits create a sense of permanence, of continuity.

Maybe at this point you are wondering, what is the difference between behaviours and habits? Let me do my best to explain. A behaviour is a *conscious* response to the different actions and situations triggered by the external environment. Habits are activities that a person does *unconsciously* in a repeated fashion. Our behaviour is a triggered response coming from our nervous system, and involves often an emotional response. Our habits are involuntary activities, that we repeatedly do, so there is no direct apparent emotion attached to it. Neurobiologists estimate that between forty to seventy percent of human behaviours can end up in habits!

That would mean that most of us go through our daily lives not really conscious about those little activities we are doing in every moment of our waking time, and to what extent those are shaping our immediate and long-term future. Daniel Coyle in his book, *The Little Book of Talent* mentions that the small actions that are performed repeatedly in a certain period of time, transform us. It is all the little things you do every day that defines who you really are.

Imagine what it would be like, if you could transform all your habits into a set of actions that are all directed towards reaching your vision! Wouldn't it be amazing? With a systematic practice, you can make it happen. The key is to do it always in small progressive steps. No one (as far as I know) can eat an entire cow in one go, but if you eat one piece of steak per day after a certain period of time you will end up eating more cows than you can actually count!

To change small habits, we can use the same approach as we did with finding out about our behaviours: Observe and identify which are those mini activities that you do every day, and detect which ones are harmful or are not helping you in the longer term to achieve your goals. A classic example: you have a nine to five job. You have built a whole routine of habits around that time schedule.

For example, you wake up around seven in the morning, take a shower, get dressed, eat breakfast, and leave your house in a hurry. You get stuck in traffic and eventually arrive to work. Around six in the afternoon, you come home, prepare dinner, watch some TV or play with your kids, and then prepare for bed. Before going to bed, you check your social media or spend the last hours of the night on the internet researching pointless stuff. Then you realise it's midnight and you need to sleep, so you force yourself to go to bed. And this same exact routine goes on from Monday to Friday. Week after week. Every Sunday you feel anxious Monday is coming again! Nothing good lasts forever and weekends are irrefutable proof.

What is wrong with that schedule? You might say: '*I need to have also my recreational time after work, right? Life cannot be all about work. I deserve my free time to do my hobbies*'. Of course, you do. But have you, for once, reflected if this schedule is the best possible way to live your life?

It seems to be the same kind of story for millions of people around the world, especially in the Western countries where working long hours is seen as something you have to do in order to advance in your career. In other cultures, like Scandinavia, the work-life balance is not measured on quantity, but rather on quality. People in Scandinavia do not need to stay long hours at work to prove their value. Ultimately, there is nothing inherently wrong with the nine to five, if you are spending your good eight work hours in a job that you really love and is taking you somewhere. The problem would be, if you are stuck in a job you don't really love, and the only motivation you have for it is the paycheck you get every month.

You know deep inside, that you would prefer to do something else. Maybe you are working as an accountant, but in reality, you would prefer to be an interior designer. Or you did a long and tedious professional study only to ding it was not your true passion, but feel obliged to get a job related to that area because otherwise, you feel it was a waste of time and money.

It's easy to fall into the trap of the never-ending rat race. To go with the collective thinking that you should do as society dictates. Most people surrender to the status quo. You end up losing the connection to your own inner voice along the way. That's why it is so important to evaluate what actions you are doing, in every single aspect of your life, and like Steve Jobs did, ask yourself the following question every morning: "If I am going to die today, would I still do what I am about to do today?" If the answer is no, too many days in a row, you know that you must change something.

To avoid procrastination, start small; start micro. I cannot repeat enough the power of doing small, incremental changes every day. You can start as simple as dedicating one hour every day for self-learning and development. Maybe you cannot change your job right away, but you can dedicate thirty minutes or one hour every day to think about what kind of job would better fit to your real aspirations, and start planning how to get there. Instead of watching one hour of Netflix every evening, you can read, or go for a walk, do some sport, or simply sit in silence and write about your plans.

You might not see the effect of these small changes right away, but after some time it will start to pay off. From all the research and observations of great leaders and successful people that I have done, I found no single individual who achieved instantaneous success or quick wins in one single go or with little effort. All of them worked incessantly, doing small things every day. With the years, the accumulated efforts had their effect: what started as a helpless seedling, grew into a power tree with roots and strength.

"Do not look for the big and quick improvement. Look for the small improvements, those that you can attack one by one. This is the only way to achieve really long term, lasting success."

- John Wooden

The Building Shape: Your Mental Models

"Each brain creates its own world, which is internally consistent and complete. Perception is not a linear process of information, reception, processing, storage and recall. Instead it is a very complex, interactive, subjective and evocative process."

- Colin Cook et al.

Our mental models define our world. Wait, what do I mean by *'mental model'*?

A mental model is a set of perceptions and assumptions that guide our behaviour and our actions. Neuroscientists believe that our perceptions are formed in the limbic system of the brain, and they contain all the external information we gathered during our lifetime; like past experiences, beliefs, past behaviours, and the environment. Based on all this information according to neuroscience, your brain creates interpretations of reality that shape the way you see and go through life.

What it is certainly not clear, is how exactly these perceptions are created in our mind? If we see our brain as the 'mechanical instrument' through which our perception gets assembled, how does the brain decide what to bring as a perception or not?

It is worthwhile giving this question a thought. What or who decides, what I pay attention to, and not? Here is the point where our intellect and our intuition may get into conflict, if we do not trust in our inner knowledge.

The mental models, or the life perceptions, are responsible for how we react in everyday situations, but most people are not really conscious about it. Many scientists believe that mental models work in an automatic fashion. That they are like part of our 'software'; they trigger the command that sustains our behaviours and execute our habits. And that basically thanks to them, we can perform the most basic activities of life.

However, there's another interesting way to look at our mental models, proposed by the great German philosopher, Immanuel Kant. He proposes in his theory of *Transcendental Idealism* that we have the conscious ability to choose our own experience and perceptions of the world. It is indeed our responsibility, to decide what perceptions we decide to bring into the awareness, even when we decide to refuse to choose. Once you choose, the machinery (our brain) runs 'automatically'. Kant emphasises that the belief in 'Free Will', God, and the immortality of the soul are the main elements that animate his ethical theory.

What does that mean for the creation of our mental models? Kant proposes that there is a metaphysical element involved; a dimension that, as humans, we cannot comprehend, but we do have a way to grasp it; which he calls sensibility. It is through sensibility that intuition is formed, and through understanding that reason enters into play. We need the combination of both to gain a cognitive perception of reality.

At this point, something worthwhile to question is, how do we know if our mental models are working in 'our favour' (in favour of our vision) or against it?

The key is observation. Being aware of your mental models and how they shape your decisions and your actions is the very first step in order to be able to change them. The idea is to bring your unconscious activities to the conscious, present moment. The best way to do it is by simply setting time for pure and simple observation. Whenever you confront yourself in a daily situation, observe your thinking patterns:

How are you feeling? How are you judging the current situation? Are you being optimistic or pessimistic?

Then ask yourself: *Is there a better way to think about this specific experience? Is it serving me towards the fulfilment of my vision? What do I have to change in myself so that I can redirect this action to the service of fulfiling my goals?*

By pure observation, you start to recognise your *paradigms*. Paradigms are simply patterns: they can be patterns of actions and patterns of thinking. We often hear that in order to make things happen the way we want them to, we need to *shift our paradigms*. This is nothing more than just observing, identifying, and deciding to change our current ways of thinking and acting so that we can redirect ourselves to wherever we want to go.

You might be wondering by now: *How do I recognise my mental models, and how does it relate to my paradigms?*

Just to make it very clear: Your mental models are *your own explanation* of your thought process and how you see the world. Simply put, it is how you have chosen to see the world, based on all the information you have gathered so far. Your paradigms are basically your action patterns: Based on what you know and believe of the world (mental model) you behave and act in certain ways (paradigms) and you achieve a certain result, which at the end represents your current reality (reinforcement of the mental model).

Let's use a simple example to illustrate how the above explanation about paradigms works. Since I was a little girl, I learned that going to school was the thing I have to do in order to be 'successful' in life; being successful in my culture, meant that I have to earn a living. I grew up with this idea implanted in my mind. At school, my teachers always talked about the importance of having a degree to function properly in society. Companies were only hiring the 'best talents' from universities; movies depicted stories of people going to school and studying hard, and they were the heroes of the story who got the better jobs in prestigious firms. The drop-offs were the rebels, the villains of the story who ended up begging for money on the streets.

I developed my own paradigm, which was in line with the external one. Because I want to earn a living and be considered successful by the society standards, I must go to school and study. I didn't question if there was another way: I simply followed unconsciously the information I had on my head, from my past experiences, and from what I heard every day. But, is this really it? Is this all I can do with my life?

What if my dream was to be an athlete, a singer, or just bake cakes? There is no doubt that going to school and studying a career is important. But isn't it worthwhile to question, whether the current school system, and universities are really serving the purpose of helping people find their own expression and their own talents and let them exploit it to the fullest? Or is our current educational scheme just an overly structured, outdated system which aims to create standardised degrees to standardise people for purposes that are definitely not at the best interest of helping people find their truest passion?

When we look at the history of education, we realise that one of the major reforms in education happened during the industrial revolution. When doing the shift from the agricultural to the industrial revolution, our way of living was profoundly affected. In the agricultural times, our lives depended on cycles of natural times and organic growth. We planned everything around the seasons. We were not interested in time-tables. With the industrial revolution, this natural rhythm got replaced by a more precise measurement of times and schedules.

As Yuval Noah Harari says it in his famous book, *Sapiens*: "The industrial revolution turned the timetable and the assembly line into a template for almost all human activities: Shortly after factories imposed their timeframes on human behaviour, schools too adopted precise timetables, followed by hospitals, government and grocery stores".

Suddenly, all our life revolves around the nine to five schedule. Not only the time schedules for schools and jobs got standardised, but also the kind of education you get in schools. Topics like creativity, sports, arts and literature were belittled by the 'serious and relevant' topics like business, engineering, and management. Who was I to question it back then as a little kid? To challenge a collective paradigm seemed unthinkable.

After recognising what mental models caused me to act and think in certain ways, I got the power to change them. That's why *observation* of your own thinking and acting patterns are the key to completely redesign your own infrastructure that building that will sustain your vision and dreams. Now, it's time to go to the next step can you guess what it is? Action!!

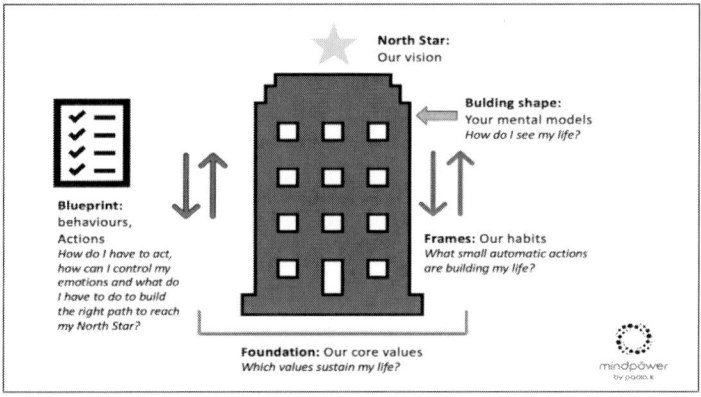

Figure 2: Design and build the infrastructure, the supportive environment to reach your vision

#TheKnechtWay to build a supportive environment to reach your vision

- To support the pathway to reach your vision, you need to build a supportive environment around it.

- The infrastructure, or supportive environment, consist of: choosing your core values (baseline), detect and modify your current behaviours if they are not serving you; re-evaluate and establish a new set of habits and finally, reshape your mental models so you can recognise the thinking pattern and open it to find new ideas.

- Pure honest observation is the key to detect and transform any behaviour, habit and thinking pattern.

- Methodical and consistent action is key to maintain the well-functioning of your vision infrastructure.

Exercises for Reflection

1. *What are your core values? How do they align with your vision?*

2. *Which behaviours have you detected in your interaction with others, are taking you away from your vision? How can you modify those behaviours?*

3. *What are the set of habits you must develop, which will support you in working every day towards your vision?*

4. *Which mental models are holding you back from acting towards reaching your vision?*

5. *How has your own education and experience affected your mental models?*

6. *Which paradigms do you need to change to make your vision happen?*

"Observation of your own thinking and acting patterns are the key to completely redesign your own infrastructure that building that will sustain your vision and dreams."

Paola Knecht

Third Pillar

Create a powerful action plan

*D*ear reader, at the time of writing these words, I'm sitting at my desk looking out my window, gazing at the beautiful trees that adorn our beloved forest which is just on the other side of the street. I've been sitting here for quite some time, thinking what is the best way I can transmit to you, how important it is to bring your plans into action.

While reviewing my notes, I found a poem that I personally like very much. I first read it in the great book from Frank Berger, *How I Raised Myself From Failure To Success In Selling*, and when I captured the essence of it, it helped me in getting a more profound understanding of what it means to take action. Sharing with you this poem is the perfect way to start our conversation around this crucial step; the third pillar of building a mindset for success.

Victory

You are the man who used to boast, that you'd achieve the uttermost someday.

You merely wished a show, to demonstrate how much you know and approve the distance you can go another year just passed through. What new ideas came to you? How many things did you do?

Time left twelve fresh months in your care, how many did you shared
with opportunity and dare, again where you so often missed?

We do not find you on the list of the makers good. Explain the fact!
Ah no, it was not the chance you lacked. You failed to Act!

- Herbert Kauffmann

It rang a bell in me when I read it. The thing is it doesn't really matter how much we think about our goals. How much time we spend on planning, and keep working on all possible paths to reach it in our head. The truth is, if we don't act on it, it will never come to life.

Action five letters that make the difference between the ones who make it and the ones who stay behind. Action is the vertebral column of every achievement. The process of doing something, to achieve an aim. Action starts in the mind and then expresses itself outward, in the external world.

What's the right way to pass from the plan to the action? For me, there is a very simple and yet very powerful way to do it: Writing your actions down! This is like bringing your thoughts to life; once they are written, they already exist somehow in the material world. Now with the right focus and activity, you can make everything happen!

Imagine: New Year's Eve. It's about to turn midnight. In my hometown, we have the ritual to wait for the new year, holding twelve grapes in a crystal glass. The grapes represent twelve goals we want to accomplish for the next year. At the twelve second countdown, you eat a grape per second. Yep, a grape per second! I used to prepare my list of wishes upfront, so that I don't have to lose time thinking of them at the countdown.

So here I am counting twelve, eleven, ten and thinking about my goals; I end up skipping some goals because thoughts don't come so fast and I don't want to have a grape choke finally three, two, one Happy New Year!! Everybody celebrates hugs, kisses, brindis the party goes on.

Everyone feels happy and energised. With every glass of prosecco, my memory of the goals that I have made some hours before starting to fade away. Suddenly, one day I open my eyes and the whole year already passed by. Twelve months later, here we are again: Holding the twelve grapes in a crystal glass. The same wishes appeared again: losing weight, finding a better job, eat healthier you name it.

What happened in the twelve previous months? They faded away so fast, and you wake up on December thirty first with the harsh reality that you did not reach any of the goals for the year. It feels like waking up from a bad hangover, right?

The power of written words

We know that nothing really happens until we take action. Yet sometimes we don't really know where to start. Over the years, I have learnt about the power of writing things down. If you have a plan in your mind and want to start taking action, the best first thing to do is to write it down! This is the best way to bring a mental idea into the material world.

If you don't write your plans and trust in your memory alone, those plans stay somewhere in the back of your mind, but you never really bring them to life, because in the struggles of daily life, you end up forgetting them, unless you have a burning passion to make things happen and then you don't really need a reminder. But for most people, we do need a reminder. We need to clear and organise our heads out, and writing our actions is one of the most therapeutic and powerful ways to get clarity on how to get what we want.

When I write things down, I feel like I am signing a contract with myself. Those things become a potential being, waiting impatiently to be brought to life. Writing my dreams, my action plans and my daily to-do lists, energises me and puts me in a positive mental state; with the simple act of writing, feels like I am actually already taking action towards my dreams.

You might be asking: *Alright, I know what are my goals, but how to I convert my goals into concrete actions so I can write them down? Where do I start?*

The very good first step, one that we often neglect, is to take the conscious *decision* to take action. There is not much science behind this. Once you take a conscious decision to act, you will put your mind and your heart to work together towards your goal.

You have already taken the first and most important steps: You have defined your vision; you understand that it requires certain behaviour and habits to get you there; you re-calibrated your mental models so they can work in favour of your goals. Now, you must define which specific actions will help you reaching them. Something that helps, is to start from the longer term, let's say, what do you want to do in next ten years from now, and then go down to middle term like, what are you going to do in five years from now, until you arrive to the now and ask yourself: what will I do today to reach the middle term goals that I set five years from now? At the end, what really matters, and what will really set you in motion, is what you are doing *right now.*

Eckhart Tolle, a spiritual teacher and author, in his book, *The Power of Now*, explains this point beautifully. "When you travel, it is very useful to know where are you going, or at least, in which direction you should go, but do not forget that the only thing that is absolutely true about your trip is the step that you are doing right now, in this moment. This is everything that is and the only thing that can be right now. *"*

It doesn't matter how small it is, a daily action will always take you further than sitting and waiting for something to happen. When you write your actions down, they become 'alive' in our brains. The step between writing it and doing it becomes easier, because every time we read it our brain registers it in a process called Encoding[1]. Thanks to this process, we are able to keep our action plan in our memories longer than if we wouldn't write them down. Of course, there are people that

---

[1] Encoding: a biological event beginning with perception through the senses. The process begins with attention, which is regulated by the thalamus and the frontal lobe, in which the memorable event causes neurons to move more frequently and so it causes that the experience seems more intense and vivid, increasing the probability of registering the event in the memory (humanmemory.net).

are more visual, or more auditive. In that case the 'writing' could also be creating a vision board, or making a recording of yourself about your goals and your action plan. Whether you create a video, a vision board or a written action plan, what matters is that you *bring it to life* in the material form so that you can keep looking at it and trigger the process to act on it.

You can download a free action planner template on the downloadable workbook on the book's website.

Tim Allen, a famous American comedian, better known for his TV show *Home Improvement* in the early nineties, has led a very successful career; but he confessed that his beginnings were very humble. He revealed to the public the method that helped him remain focused on his career while working himself up to the top. He basically maintains three lists which are based in the logic explained previously: In the first list, he writes down the goals he wants to achieve in his life. In the second list, he writes all the things he needs to do this year in order to reach his life goals. In the third list, he writes what he needs to do today in order to reach his life goals. The key of maintaining this method up and running is *discipline.* We will explore more in detail about how to develop an extraordinary self-discipline in the sixth pillar.

What holds us back from action?

So far it is clear that if you want to be successful at any endeavour, action is crucial. But what is it that holds us back from the famous promotional Nike phrase, *Just do it?*

We associate the word 'action' with 'fight'

Many of us relate indirectly the word 'action' with some sort of fighting. During my coaching sessions, I have realised that when I ask the question *"What holds you back from doing what you want to do?"* I have got the same sort of answers from my clients many times: *"I am afraid to start looking for a new job. I will have to fight and compete with many others to get a chance of an interview"*- or *"I am afraid to open a new business because I have to fight for customers with many others that are already in the market and what if I fail?"*

Somehow, people relate the word 'action' with fight and potential pain. It's in our nature to look for sources of pleasure and avoid the pain. When we delay a decision or an action, what we are really doing is delaying a potential sensation of pain; then we use our thought process in a way that justifies our delay in the action. Procrastination becomes a tool to avoid pain, with the side effect that procrastination often results in no-action at all.

The word 'fighting' for sure does not bring much pleasure when we hear it; but not all fighting is as negative as we think it is. In fact, according to the latest neurological studies, when it comes to creativity and talent development, the process of fighting is not an option, but a biological necessity to build new neurological connections in our brain.

The pain and frustration that we experience when we keep doing things and 'fail', is the result of forcing the limits of our current capacity: Our brain needs to come to this limit point, this 'limit line' that feels like we almost make it but fall short; at this point, our brain triggers a response of building more brain connections; which will get reinforced every time we repeat the action until it becomes part of who we are. Professor Robert Bjork from UCLA university points it rightly: "The brain works like any other body muscle: There is no gain when there is no pain".

So, every time you think about how painful it is to act, remember this: The pain you experience when confronting yourself to challenging situations is necessary for success! Taking responsibility for confronting your actions is an act of transcendence; where you start to think beyond what is visible and attainable, to the invisible and the potential that emerges in making something become a possibility.

How to identify the right actions?

So far, we talked about how important it is to write an action plan, and how to avoid procrastination by understanding that any effort invested in your actions brings results. But how can we define the right actions?

Remember, it's easier to eat a piece of steak per day than to attempt to eat the whole cow in one sitting. So, it's important to work on your action plan in the same way you did when defining your habits and behaviours to sustain your vision: Start from the general (strategic, long term) to the specifics (short term, daily). If you work systematically from the general to the specific, you can detect easily which actions do not make sense for your goal (vision), and which ones do make sense.

Do not forget to listen to your intuition when you are in the process of defining your actions. Does it feel right for you? Will this action or set of actions will take you to where you want to be? Try to identify which actions you have defined based on your own inner desire and which ones have a more "external" reason. As Jack Cranfield says: "Everything you think, say and do needs to become intentional and aligned with your purpose, your values and your goals."

Remain vigilant of your actions. Observe them every day. You can get easily off the tracks when you do not review them consistently. Remember: habits are powerful. The wrong set of habits will lead you to the wrong actions. Maintain a vigilant mode. Even if you don't think about it, a small deviation of your plan, can lead you to a whole differ-ent place if you don't detect the deviation and correct it. If we use the same analogy of the airplane: If you want to go to New York, but your plane deviates one mile every minute, you will end up somewhere com-pletely different, maybe in another continent!

"Vision without action is merely a dream. Action without vision just passes the time. Vision with action can change the world."

- Joel A. Barker

You have control only about three things in your life: Your thoughts, your feelings, and your actions. How you use those three determines everything you will experience in life.

ACTION:

Let's check your mood at the moment. How are you feeling today?

Write two immediate actions you can do right now that will make you feel instant happiness. Don't forget to share it with me on socials using the hashtag #SuccessWithKnecht

Persistence: The magic ingredient for success

I can bet you a hundred that the following has happened to you: You have been very enthusiastic about starting a project; maybe you want to lose weight, or start a new business, or to bring order in your house. The motivation and energy in the beginning feels great, so you have a great start in your project. Then, two or three weeks passed and you start to realise you aren't getting results. Your energy levels and motivation start to fall every day that passes and you keep seeing zero results. Then, you have a conversation about it with your best buddy; you tell her how disappointed you feel about your results. Then she answers you, after sipping her cup of tea, with the infamous words: *"Well my friend ... don't give up, keep going!"*. You feel disappointed about this answer. *"Really, you cannot think of something better to tell me than this cliché?"* you reply or at least you think about it.

'Never give up'- we hear it so often we take for granted the powerful meaning of it. Action alone does not guarantee success. It is a big first step, but eventually what takes people farther than they thought possible is persistence and continuous action.

The reality is that most people give up too soon on their dreams. As soon as the first failures appear, they start questioning if it's the right thing to do. The fear of losing money, relationships, reputation, ends up dominating their minds and eventually they abandon their dream they stop that business, throw away that book proposal, stop training you name it.

But I tell you something that experience has taught me: To achieve anything worthwhile in this life, requires a constant commitment and focus. I see persistence as the key vital element to keep your vision alive. You can be very talented, resourceful and design great action plans, but if you don't persist on them, they will never happen.

73

Jack Ma is one of the richest men in Asia and in the world, with a net worth of forty-three billion dollars at the time of writing. His personal story is one of the best living examples about how persistence can bring you literally from zero to hero.

Jack had a very humble beginning. He lived with his family in his natal town Hangzhou, China. During his childhood time, he spent a lot of his time learning English. He liked to ride his bike twenty-seven kilometres to a local hotel where he offered tours to the tourists in exchange for getting to practice his English.

Since the very early years of his life, Jack has been confronted by a great number of rejections and failures of all kinds. Even when trying to get an education, he had a bumpy ride as he failed the entry school tests multiple times.

Things didn't get any better with time: When wanting to enter university, he also failed the entry exam. Then he had the idea to apply to Harvard, and got rejected ten times.

Failure also met Jack when trying to get a job. He said in several interviews that he applied to over thirty jobs with no success. Some of those jobs were quite odd, like the time he applied to become a police officer: "*you are not good*" was their answer, when Jack tried to get in.

There is a popular story, about Jack trying to get into KFC when the famous chain came to China: "*twenty-four people applied for a job in KFC. Twenty three got the job, I wasn't one of them* "

In 1995, Jack met some colleagues at his modest apartment in his natal Hangzhou, to talk about a business idea. He saw the possibility to develop an online platform that would support small suppliers spread all over the country to buy and sell their goods. At that time, e-commerce was virtually non-existent in China.

Although Jack Ma went through many difficulties and hardships, he managed to keep focused and persistent. He handled every rejection with patience and came up with new ways to solve problems. Alibaba, became after ten years of its foundation, one of the most successful e-commerce platforms worldwide.

Ma has been asked on several occasions what has been the key to his success. He always mentions the word *persistence.*

"Just keep going. Persistence is necessary. Today is very difficult, to-morrow is difficult, but the day after tomorrow is very beautiful."

- Jack Ma

Never give up. The sentence suddenly makes a lot of sense when you put it into a context like this, doesn't it?

Persistent action vs. letting go where are the limits?

We understand that persistence combined with consistent action is an important 'ingredient' for success; but where does our intuition fit in all of this? What are the limits between performing conscious action based on intellect, versus listening to our intuition and letting ourselves be guided by it?

It is worthwhile remembering that everything we do, must be connected to our vision. Persistence is a wonderful thing to develop in order to achieve the things we want; however, parrot persistence without the guidance of our highest will, becomes merely an intellectual, mechanical concept that lacks real meaning.

Perhaps the spiritual author, Michael Bernard Beckwith acknowledged this fact when he said, "Pain will push you until the vision pulls you". Once you have a very clear view about your vision, what is very important is to go through your journey taking care of each step along the way. Keep your sights on the final destination, but focusing mainly on the immediate steps to follow at the present moment. The persistence that results in following each step, doing one thing at a time, with the attention completely turned to the present instead of on the intended result, is what makes the real success come to pass.

One of the main struggles of our human nature is that we become overly stressed by letting our intellect put enormous amount of effort in trying to solve our problems, blocking the natural creative mechanism that already exist within us. Dr Maxwell Maltz, refers to this point by arguing that "Our trouble is that we ignore the automatic creative mechanism and try to do everything and solve all our problems by conscious thought or forebrain thinking".

According to Dr Maltz, the real success comes from an act of surrender: "The way to success, vouched for by innumerable personal narrations, is by surrender passivity, not activity - relaxation, not intentness, should be now the rule. Give up the feeling of responsibility, let go your hold, resign the care of your destiny to higher powers, be genuinely indifferent of what it comes of it all it is but giving your private convulsive a rest, and finding that the greater Self is there".

Many of us do not see ourselves as being creative beings; We think that being creative belongs to the artist, the philosophers, the writers people "out of the normal reach". But if you really think about it, every single human being is creative. Being creative is the natural state of manhood, this is our God-given gift. Most people remain blind or ignorant to this fact because the creative capacity can only operate in the present, which is the permanent state of our existence. When we stop and think about something, we trigger the past or the future; in those arenas the creative mind cannot operate, because it is pure fiction. This is the arena of the intellect. If we stop thinking, we let our creative Self space act spontaneously. In short, to be spontaneous, is to be creative.

In the story of Jack Ma we could read implicitly that one of the things that kept him going despite all the difficulties encountered was his endless persistence in following his dream and the act of listening to his inner GPS (aka intuition).

Now that we know that following our intuition along with persistence is what makes all the difference, I can sense that you might have the following question: How can I get *conscious* about my inner intuition *modus operandi*? Is there a way to get answers from it in a conscious way?

The answer is Yes! And it is through guess how?

Easy. By asking your intuition directly!

Asking the right questions to trigger action

"What is the meaning of life I came to a conclusion that what really matters is trying to understand the right questions to ask and the more we can increase the scope and scale of human consciousness the better we are able to ask these questions."

- Elon Musk

"Ask, and it will be given to you; seek, and you will find; knock, and it will be opened to you."

- Mathew 7:7

Our thinking process is the mysterious and fascinating act of asking ourselves questions and answering them all the time. Directly and indirectly, the questions we make to ourselves are shaping our thoughts, the attitude we assume, and the actions that we perform. Questions are the fundamental pillar of our learning process.

The difference between people who have had success in their lives and the ones who have not, is that the first ones asked themselves better questions and as a consequence, got better answers.

Think about the type of questions you are asking yourself every day. Are they leading you towards doing positive action or rather they are holding you back?

For example, when you are confronted with failure; let's say that you applied for a job you really wanted and did not get it. What do you ask to yourself after receiving the news? Do you ask, *"Why did this happen to me?"*, *"What did I do wrong?"*, those questions will seek for an answer, and you will find it. Your own thought process will look for answers that validify the sentiment of failure and hopelessness, which indirectly you are seeking. Those answers will then lead to a chain of negative thoughts that will reinforce again and again asking similar demotivating kind of questions and will produce similar, demotivated answers and similar mediocre results.

What if instead, you ask better questions? For example, if you don't get the job, you can ask yourself: *"What have I learned from this experience? What things I need to improve to have a better performance next time? How can I get my next great opportunity?* Asking those questions will definitely take you to a new whole direction. It will focus your mental energy in finding solutions leading you to take a different kind of action and getting different results.

Asking yourself the right questions, will determine everything you do in your life.

Let's take another example. Think about which kind of questions you are asking yourself in relation to your personal finances. When you receive your salary, or some income, what is the first question you ask to yourself? Do you ask: *'In what can I spend this money now?'* Or rather: *'How can I make a good financial plan to make grow this money?'* The kind of question will give you the answer that reinforces the question and your action will be driven by those answers. Be very careful about what you are asking to yourself!

The questions we ask to ourselves should have three specific functions: They should be focused, relevant and resourceful. Let's look at those functions with specific examples:

1. *The questions you ask yourself should help you to see where to put your focus:* not only is important that the question is constructive; you also shall seek for the solution that brings better results. For example, if you ask yourself *"How can I feel happier right now?"* and the first answer that comes back is *"There is nothing you can do"*, keep insisting. Do not settle for the first answer. Persist in asking, and the true desire of the question will lead to a better answer!

2. *The questions should point out what we suppress:* In a world where we can access millions of bits of information a day, our mind performs the heroic act of focusing on the information that we really need to perform optimally. So, it all depends where do you redirect your questions. For example, if you ask yourself *"Why do I feel so bad today?"*, the mind will come up with all possible reasons why you feel awful and will suppress

everything that would make you feel good. The mind brings back to your consciousness what you directly ask!

3. *Questions help us find resources we will utilise*: One day after a difficult day at work, I felt depleted. I had no energy left. All I wanted was to watch some TV and go to bed. However, later that night I had scheduled to study for a very important certification exam that would mean a lot to me. I had two options; one was to ask myself the following questions: *"Why do I have to still study after a long day? Why don't I deserve a little bit of fun and rest? Why do I never have time for myself?"* Those questions came to my mind for sure, but I could detect them, and decided to ask myself better questions. So, I kept asking: *"What can I do now to get more energy and go to study? What will happen if I go to study and I pass the exam? How will passing the exam improve my life later?"*

In a matter of minutes, I felt a new energy. I started to imagine myself feeling like a winner because I started to build mental images about what great things will come because I passed the exam. I felt so excited and willing, that I even went to study before the scheduled time I set up for myself. That's where for the first time I tested the power of questions and how amazingly effective they are in shaping your life.

Make yourself questions that will help you go towards your goals. Those questions that elevate your human spirit and demand a better answer. Great questions demand great answers. Instead of focusing on finding excuses why you cannot do something, invest that precious time in making the right questions: *What can you do now, that will help in getting where you want to go? What do you have to change in yourself to make it happen? How can you become a better person, parent, professional?* Do not settle for good go for the excellent!

"What is important is to never stop asking. The curiosity has its own reason of existing: One cannot help but feeling stunned when you contemplate the mysteries of eternity, of life, and the wonderful structure of reality. It is enough if one tries to learn a bit of life's mystery every day. Never lose your saint curiosity."

- Albert Einstein

#TheKnechtWay to take powerful action

- Taking action is the only way you will accomplish what you wish for;

- Write your actions down to boost the powerful effect it brings to your mind and to your subconscious;

- Structure your action plan in a way that makes it easier to act one step at a time: Go for life goals, down to yearly goals, down to monthly and daily goals;

- Persistent and continuous action focused on the present, is the magic ingredient for success;

- Your creative Self can only manifest itself by acting spontaneously in the present moment; if you "stop and think" about solutions, your intellect takes the lead and suppresses the creative Self.

- To trigger the best possible action from your creative Self, ask yourself the right questions;

- Our own life is the result of all the questions we have made and the answers we decided to act on;

- If you realise that you are making negative or non-useful questions, make a conscious effort to make to yourself constructive, valuable and challenging questions that will guide you to constructive, valuable and worthwhile results.

Exercises for Reflection:

1. *Define what are the main actions you need to do in your life to achieve your vision*

2. *What are the main barriers stopping you from taking action in getting what you want?*

3. *What kind of questions are you asking yourself every morning? Are they inspiring or depressing?*

4. *What are you asking yourself every night before going to bed? Did you achieve today what you wanted to achieve?*

5. *What can you do right now, in the next few minutes, that will take you more towards the direction of your dreams?*

"Our own life is the result of all the questions we have made and the answers we decided to act on."

Paola Knecht

Fourth Pillar

Don't be a Perfectionist Strive for Excellence

"If you look for perfection, you will never be content."

- Leo Tolstoy

In our society, we praise perfectionism. We think of being perfect as the highest aim: We must have a perfect body, a perfect intelligence. A perfect house, a perfect family and perfect experiences in short, we aim for the perfect Hollywood tale kind of life.

You don't need to look very far: As soon as you get into social media, you see the effects perfectionism has on people. Everybody wants to show their best image, their perfect side.

At the same time, odd enough, when something does not go as expected, when we fall short behind the 'being perfect' standard, we also realise the fact that perfection is an unattainable goal. When we make a mistake, people tell us, 'Well, nobody is perfect'. So, we acknowledge the fact, but we still feel terrible if we don't reach the bar of perfection. You may agree with me, that the whole idea about perfectionism is confusing. On one side, we venerate the collective view of perfectionism and accept it as an aspiring goal. On the other side, when we fail, we tend to justify our shortcomings by saying that perfection does not exist.

Perfectionism seems to me like a slavish concept. An imaginary place to hide when we are too afraid to take responsibility for our actions. We hide our vulnerability, and our true selves from being hurt, and prefer to wait until reaching 'perfection': Like a lonely fairy tale princess waiting at the top of the tower for the perfect prince that will rescue her, marry her and bring her to a happily ever after.

We also tend to associate perfectionism with success. If we do things perfectly, then we should be rewarded, we should be successful in our endeavours. This association can be very dangerous. First of all, we cannot aim for perfection when we don't understand the foundations of what it means to be perfect. To be perfect in the eyes of everybody is obviously an impossibility, something unattainable. When you set yourself unattainable goals with no real foundation but a mere abstract belief of perfection, you will suffer.

Perfectionism is an imaginary place coming from the ego. It comes from our intense fear of being judged and our internal insecurity of not feeling good enough. It is an attempt to procrastinate action; it blocks creativity and the possibility to use your intuition.

You may argue that some degree of perfectionism is good; that there is nothing bad in wanting to do the things the best possible way you are able to do it. I fully agree with that, but there is a difference between trying to do everything perfect, and trying to do things the best possible way. I believe the latter involves your heart, your focus, your effort your willingness to do what it takes, to perform the best that is possible, regardless of the outcome or what others think. There is a difference between perfectionism and striving for excellence.

So, you might be thinking that both terms 'perfectionism' and 'striving for excellence' sound very similar. What is then the difference?

What makes perfectionism a bad thing to follow and excellence the good thing to aim for?

In short, if you want to reach a state of perfection, then there is no more place to grow. If you think you will arrive at perfection, your life will be perfect and everything will be great, then you miss the chance to keep growing. To strive for excellence recognises the fact that you can improve yourself in an unlimited way: You can strive to do the best you possibly can, and you will keep learning along the way.

According to the Cambridge Dictionary, excellence means *excelling at something*. It means greatness; to become the very best. It's possessing high qualities in a high degree. It requires practice, dedication and devotion; it's something that only through intense practice and hard work you can attain. Excellence in my opinion, is connected to acts of love. It's a quality you develop from the inside.

Perfectionism, on the other side, is not something that comes from love, from the inside. It comes from the external expectations of other people, of societies or entities, whether you consciously know it or not. It has a set of unrealistic expectations and predetermined definitions. It comes from the need to be accepted and liked, to belong. It fulfils the collective ego, and not your inner nature. That's why it is unattainable: it is nearly impossible to please everybody all the time.

If you really want to be successful, then aiming for excellence is the way to go. To become excellent in what you do, in what you want to offer to the society and the world, aligns with your vision and passion. You wouldn't want to become excellent at something you are not passionate about, would you?

How do you know that you are being a perfectionist instead of aiming for excellence?

In short, an easy way to detect if you are being a perfectionist is when:

- You feel very anxious about the results
- You are afraid of how other people will judge you and see you
- The idea of perfection comes from an external source: Your family, co-workers, the media, your friends, society
- No matter how much you work, it seems never good enough
- You think more on the final reward than the process of getting there: Money, success, popularity, etc.
- You feel afraid to act; you always doubt before doing the next steps
- You get very frustrated and angry if things do not go as expected

Now on the other side, when you are aiming to be excellent in your actions, you will most likely:

- Feel energised every time you are doing the activity
- Have an inner motivation to act the best way you possibly can
- Feel that what you are aiming at is connected with your vision
- Feel like this is a continuous learning process, with no real end
- Have a sense that you are contributing to build something greater than yourself
- Feel that you are learning a lot about yourself- your strengths and weaknesses

In short, perfectionism does not lead to self-improvement. It comes from the primary thought of trying to get approval from external sources. The main question you ask yourself is: *What will they think?* A healthy action of striving for excellence involves the question: *What can I do better, how can I keep improving?*

ACTION:

Are you being a perfectionist? Do you want to get more strategies about how to overcome perfectionism behaviour? Look for additional tips and exercises you can get for free by accessing my booklet in the book's website.

Perfection paralyzes achievement

When I was in high school, my literature teacher exhorted us to join a poetry contest. You had to submit a poem of your creation within the assigned deadlines and if your poem qualified, you would be selected to compete in a national contest. My love for words was undeniable already at that time, and I loved to write short poems as a teenager. The possibility to show a poem of my creation to the public seemed to me exciting but at the same time it filled me with panic; *"What if they think my poems are ridiculous?"*, *"What if people start laughing when I present my poem in the podium*? Of course, I was asking myself all the wrong questions.

Despite my fear, I decided to participate. I pre-selected one of my favourite poems, one I dedicated to my father, who passed away when I was eleven years old. When the deadline to submit the poem approached, I started to get very nervous. I started to doubt whether my poem was good enough to get submitted.

As a consequence of my nervousness, I started to scratch some sentences, replace them with others I started to turn around some proses. I read it and re-read it. I tried to rebuild it. It never looked good enough. I started to feel ashamed of myself. I thought my poem was not yet perfect. I thought my teacher and colleagues would laugh at me. The deadline passed by and I couldn't submit my poem. I decided to keep the poem for myself.

My professor tried to convince me to submit what I had but I just couldn't do it. The fear of shame was bigger than my desire to show it to the public. I never made it to the contest.

Some years later, I found the original poem in one of my old journals I kept during high school. It reminded me of a remote lost opportunity.

What if I had submitted it, and won? I would probably have chosen a very different path life than I did at the time. I will never know, because I lost that opportunity.

However, the whole experience was not a complete loss. I learned something very powerful: I promised to myself that no matter what happens, I will never lose a chance again. Even if the first attempt doesn't work, I will try it a second time, a third time all the time it takes and I will learn from each failure every time.

Because the pain of failing gets more bearable and even can disappear over time, but the pain of never having tried something stays with you forever.

Looking back at this experience, I understood that my inner motivation of not exposing my poem to the class had to do with my feelings of perfectionism. I was too afraid that my poem would not be 'perfect' to the eyes of others.

Since the poem is a creation coming from my heart, the vulnerability I felt by exposing something so close to my deepest feelings felt terrifying. If I would have acted thinking primarily about the experience of writing a poem and the desire to get better at it, I would have acted different. I would have seen this as an opportunity to get feedback and get better at it, and I would have felt more enthusiastic about exposing it with others, even if I felt a bit nervous or anxious. Eventually, the desire to share it and get better would have had more influence on me that the fear of not having a perfect poem from the start.

Brené Brown, in her book, *Dare to Lead* describes very clearly the detrimental effects of being a perfectionist: "Perfectionism is a self-destructive and addictive belief system that fuels this primary thought: If I look perfect and do everything perfectly, I can avoid or minimise the painful feelings of shame, judgement and blame. Perfectionism is self-destructive because it does not exist. It's an unattainable goal. Perfectionism is more about perception than an internal motivation".

There is just one thing about being perfect that I regard as the truth: The nature of our existence, our bodies and our minds are perfect by design. We have been designed in a perfect way by our Creator. Perfectionism is a human-made concept, a collective superfluous definition that discriminates the perfection of all that exists, and gives credit to a very narrowed view of how the world should be and how humanity should be. Only by being curious and exploring life and all its unlimited expressions is how we can discover it and stay in tune with it; that is in my perspective the best way to strive for excellence.

The path towards excellence

"We are what we repeatedly do. Excellence, therefore, is not an act,
but an habit."

- Aristotle

When we look at the most successful people in the world, they all are extraordinarily good at something. They seem to be calm, cheerful, ethereal, as if they are supernatural beings. We see their achievements as if like the hand of God had intervened; so precise and perfect: The symphonies of Mozart, the peaceful and coordinated protests involving millions of people towards non-violence organised by Gandhi, the grandeur of the speeches of Winston Churchill, the perfect, beautiful and harmonious performance of the prima ballerina Ana Pavlova. From the outside, it looks like they were born with that talent, and they did nothing for it, but nothing could be further from the truth.

I do believe that there are people that are born with prodigious talents and so everything they do looks natural and spontaneous. But that doesn't mean that they have always become successful at their craft. It requires constant practice, confrontation with failures, frustrations and a very strong discipline and work ethic, to achieve something big and transcendental.

We might not see the amount of effort, failure, frustration and work that those people we consider geniuses and gurus spent in mastering their skill. Tom Brady, considered one of the best American football players of all times, has mentioned in several interviews that he follows a very strict diet in a very meticulous way and has a workout routine for at least five hours a day for five days a week to keep himself in top shape.

He has become the first player in NFL history to win seven Super Bowl championships, the last most recent won at age forty-three at the time of writing. That he was gifted in sports, gave him an advantage of course. But what really took him to the top of his game was his discipline, his consistency and above all, a full commitment to working hard. In a recent interview, Brady recognised that he has less natural talent than many pro quarterbacks, so he has to work harder than others.

"The only thing that I know, is to go out there and work at it. I'm not buying into any hype or potential. I'm into work."

- Tom Brady

Socrates once said: "The highest form of human excellence is to question oneself and others". Keep learning, keep alert to feedback, and always look for ways to improve and be excellent!

Be authentic

When you meet a person for the first time, what makes you trust that first impression of them? Is it their looks, voice, or posture? All of the above?

Has it happened to you that you meet someone, and you feel this person is very special? That she has like a magnet, a charm, something non-descriptively pleasant? You feel the need to see this person again, or feel you would like to know this person more?

I have. And when I reflect about what is it that makes him or her so special, I come to the conclusion that this person felt authentic to me. I could connect on a deeper level because that channel of synchronization was open; I call this trust, and the source of trust is the truth.

I believe people have on a deeper level a sixth sense to recognise when someone is being authentic and who is not. And this is often reflected in the first impressions.

Being authentic is hard in our current society. It means to show yourself in the open, regardless of what others might think of you. It means to go beyond the comfort zone of playing the 'nice, well-mannered person' and display wildly your own persona.

You cannot strive for excellence when you are not telling the truth about yourself. You might reach higher positions in a hierarchical status at work or in a social circle, but it will be a weak construction, something that will fall apart very easily the moment someone tries to blow you off.

Being excellent means being authentic.

Being true to yourself and true to others about your intentions, and about who you are.

We admire leaders and successful people because we believe they display their truth on the highest level. They open up their desires and true intentions for you to grab and experience as well. Just think for a moment about a person you really admire. What do you admire about him or her in particular?

Most of the times, you admire them because they display a truth that you identified with. For example, one of my most admired leaders, as I already mentioned, is Nelson Mandela. I admire him because I identify in him the fire of persistence and of never giving up for his dream, something I recognise in myself as well and consider it as truth. I admire as well my first boss that I had at my corporate job. She was kind, smart, polite but strong, and always had the best interest of the team at the core of her heart. You could see it, immediately. She didn't have to give great speeches, be political, or promise too much. She just had to be herself for you to fully trust her.

Being authentic should be easy, not hard. If we allow ourselves to get out from the imaginary cave of our egos, things will flow more easily in life.

Try it out. Stand straight up, speak up. Command respect, and let yourself flow. Life rewards those who have the courage to speak their truth.

Wait a second. I can sense that you might still have some unanswered questions

Are you perhaps wondering how can you know if you are being true to yourself or not? How could you possibly find out?

Here starts to get more exciting. We discussed in the previous pillar, that our creative higher Self, can only operate freely when we stay present in the moment. We also discussed that our intuition comes from the act of being spontaneous; and that being spontaneous only works when we are focused in the present moment. Can you see the relationship?

Being authentic = Let the creative Self operate in the present moment. That basically is the same as saying 'act spontaneously'. If you want to access the creative Self, then leave the 'stop and think' out of the way which that belongs to the past and/or future, which does not exist. You cannot be in the truth when you are not in the present. Can you see it now?

"80% of our mental activity is irrelevant, expendable, even counter-productive. It is much healthier to trust your intuition, the first impulse. Reflections almost never move us towards action; most of them move us towards paralysis."

Pablo d'Ors

#TheKnechtWay to strive for excellence

Remember that perfectionism is a self-destructive behaviour that paralyzes action:

- Perfectionism comes from a constant fear of being judged and not being 'good enough' for others.

- Being perfect according to society standards, is an unattainable goal, therefore it leads to anger, frustration and even depression.

- Striving for excellence is not the same as trying to be perfect. To aspire to excellence is to recognise that there are infinite ways to improve and it takes discipline and hard work to get there.

- To be excellent at something is a desire fueled by a deeper meaning inside of you: Your love and your passion towards the activity you want to be excellent at.

- Authenticity is the gate that takes you towards excellence.

- Being true to yourself is a must, if you want to grow and transcend in life.

- Being true to yourself means: Trust your creative Self, which operates only in the present moment. In other words: Act spontaneously!

Exercises for Reflection:

1. *Think about an achievement you have had recently and you feel proud of. How did you make it happen?*

2. *What does excellence mean to you? Think about an important project that you need to complete. How can you apply the concept of excellence to complete it in the most successful way?*

3. *Observe your daily activities. Are you giving your best in each situation? Every time you have completed a specific task, ask yourself, is this the best possible way I can do it, or can I do it better?*

4. *What are five things you can improve right now about yourself?*

5. *What is your truth? Describe three daily situations where you can display your truth at best*

"Only by being curious and exploring life and all its unlimited expressions is how we can discover it and stay in tune with it; that is in my perspective the best way to strive for excellence."

Paola Knecht

Fifth Pillar

Confront the Fear of Failure

*H*ave you heard the saying *"Tell me what you fear and I will tell you who you are?"*

Believe or not, your fears can be the gate that conducts you to your real passion, to your real nature.

How could that be possible? Stay tuned.

Have you asked yourself, what fear really is? If we look at the standard definition, you will find things like *"Fear is an emotion that is characterised by an intense sensation of discomfort caused by a potential danger- real or imaginary. It can be manifested in the present or it can even be triggered by something that happened in the past or for what will happen in the future"*.

In scientific terms, researchers that study the effects of fear focuses on the biological and physical effects we experiment once the fear sensation dominates the human mind: First the object of fear is decoded by the brain; the information goes through the limbic system, which then starts to trigger survival reactions like the fighting mode and escape mechanisms.

At all moments, the limbic system is registering perceptions and keeps adjusting the reactions to maintain the alert state even during our sleep.

Once our limbic system detects and registers the potential danger, the amygdala triggers a series of answers which travel through our body and alerts it to react against the potential danger. Some reactions our body experiments are as follows:

- Increase of blood pressure;
- Increase of muscular tension;
- Increase of adrenaline;
- Increase of glucose levels on the blood;
- Supression of non-essential body functions.

The reaction to fear can be so intense, that it could even turn us into a panic mode, which is a very intense fear sensation, where you could lose bodily control partially or even completely.

The scientific conception of fear described above makes perfect sense when we talk about the preservation instincts that most creatures have. When a creature is directly exposed to a dangerous situation, its first reaction is to fight towards protecting his life.

What is really curious about humanity is that we experiment fear not only on the physical plane but also on the psychological one: We can experience fear to thoughts from experiences in the past or imaginary situations. When this is the case, our reaction mechanism is also a very interesting one: instead of triggering us into action, it paralyzes us.

This sensation of incapability or paralysis towards a potential fear is what make us feel vulnerable. Vulnerability is nothing more than the feeling of powerlessness: the belief of being incapable of dealing with difficult or risky situations, uncertainty and physical and/or emotional exposure.

But why does this happen? Why do we feel so fearful to thoughts that happened in the past or might happen in the future?

If you stop and think too much, you are not in the present. The fear experienced is an imaginary entity living in the past or in the future. Thus, fear is the lack of identification with your true Self. When the perception of who you are is just linked with the judgement of the information you gather from the outside, with your past, experiences and opinions of others, you start to lose contact with the inside. If the information from the outside contains mainly negative feedback, and you accept it as 'the truth', the brain cortex will record this information to trigger a defence reaction in your body: you start to feel ashamed, scared and you take the decision to keep yourself in a safe place.

Brené Brown emphasised the danger of feeling ashamed in her book *Dare to Lead*: "Shame keep us small, resentful and afraid. In Shame-prone cultures, where parents, leaders, and administrators consciously or unconsciously encourage people to connect their self-worth to what they produce, I see disengagement, blame, gossip, stagnation, favouritism and a total dearth of creativity and innovation".

"So we can go as far as to say that Fear is the real killer of creativity."

Paola Knecht

Knowing that fear and shame is so detrimental for living not only the life of our dreams, but to live a healthy and balanced life, I wonder: What keeps people motivated to surrender to their fears?

Everybody could probably answer that question for themselves; my answer, the one that speaks to my heart is the following: We surrender to our fears when we live in the state of non-truth. We are afraid when we are *disconnected*: from the world and its wonders, from other people, from our communities and heritages, from our own nature from our present.

How to reconnect back to the world and its infinite wonders definitely deserves a separate book. For the purpose of this book, I will focus on two major sources of fear that are fundamental to take a look at: Disconnection from people and disconnection from our own truth.

Reconnecting back with people

Dealing with negative feedback

Everybody panics at the potential 'no' as an answer. It's so scary that most people prefer not to do something meaningful for them if this exposes them to hear those two terrible letters.

Much work has been published about how to deal with negative feedback. There are countless techniques about how to deal with rejection in general. However, no matter how much you read and investigate about the topic; the true fact of life is that if you want to be successful at anything, you have to get used to it. You have to embrace the word 'no' and take it as a given. The best thing to do is to ignore it. It might be frightening in the beginning. But as everything in life, the more you practice it, the better you get at it.

There are millions of reasons why someone will say 'no' to you. The vast majority of those reasons will be something that has nothing to do with you as a person. In most cases, it will be that somebody says no to you because he or she is in bad mood; had other self-interests; it was a rainy day; the paycheck didn't come; the partner left them you name it. So, to act to somebody's no as a life sentence is complete nonsense.

The best thing you can do when you hear the word next time, is to ignore it and concentrate your thinking in how to convert the 'no' into a 'yes' in your next move. Focus your energy on the next steps and keep going!

Life is a delicate balance. Being persistent does not mean dealing with the same rejection over and over again just for the sake of it. You should handle persistence in a smart way. That means that you keep your eyes open and look for other ways to reach what you want to accomplish. The key is to find a balance between being persistent and learning to move forward when you don't see progress after a while. Unfortunately, there is no cookie-cutter technique to reach this balance. It is all a matter of trial and error and learn from your experience. With the time, you will develop your gut and you will be able to do it more intuitively.

In the meantime, accumulate enough no's to hit the next yes!

"Do you believe in yourself and the things you want to do? Are you prepared for many setbacks and failures? Whatever your calling may be, each error, each failure is like a strike-out. Your greatest asset is the number of strike outs you have had since your last hit. The greater the number, the nearer you are to your next hit."

– Frank Bettger

Learning to say no

There are times when you need to be very careful with what you commit to do for others. Living in a social environment, it's common that you receive many requests from people as a form of looking for help, advice, or that you do something for them. If you want to maintain control over your time and resources, saying no will be your best ally.

Just as we have to learn to deal with rejections from others, we also need to learn to reject people, activities and duties that are not in line with our priorities and goals. We need to get comfortable in saying no to things we know that are not adding any value to our life.

Imagine: It's Friday, 6:00 pm. You are finishing up some last affairs from work before you hit the weekend. You have an important event this evening: It's your wedding anniversary. You promised your partner to be on time and pick up a cake on the way home. Suddenly, you receive a call from your boss; He needs a very important report and asks you to complete it within the next hour. You say: *"Of course, I will work on it right away and you will have the report on your email within an hour"*. Then you hang up the phone and realise you are screwed. You will be late for the wedding anniversary celebration and will need to arrange for someone else picks up the cake. Sound familiar? Most people will painfully nod their heads. When reviewing your values, you know that family is your priority, but the fear to say no to your boss paralyzed you and you were unable to respond how you really wanted.

Saying no to others is as important as to handle the 'no' from others. Human affairs are an art, and we might not always get it right. But if you act with a strong conviction and with your values and priorities clear, then it doesn't matter who you upset. What matters is that you stay true to yourself, because that's what will bring you the real success.

Become a master of dealing with people

In the modern world, being afraid is rarely a matter of a physical life or death situation, but it has to do more with something psychological. I can go as far to say, that most of our source of fear nowadays is from living in an increasingly interconnected, fast-paced social environment, which means that we have to deal with an increasing amount of people, often coming from a different culture and/or country, which make us feel more vulnerable and insecure.

If I reflect on the reasons why people feel vulnerable and insecure towards other people, I tend to refer back to myself and try to understand it from my own perspective. When I have experienced that fear, it has been often related to a situation where I needed to obtain something or share something with people that I don't normally know.

If I have to give a speech to a group of people, or need to ask for a difficult or special task to someone, I get a sort of feeling of inconvenience, I feel anxious, a subtle but present feeling that makes me question if I am not sufficient or adequate to perform that task. And so, two things can happen, the first being that I might decide to back off and don't do it or delay it; or the second, I think about what I can offer them of value and still decide to do it despite my fear because I see it as necessity and I cannot get away without doing it.

Sometimes, the fear of being judged and ridiculed is so strong that we often forget that we are dealing with another human being: People that most likely feel as insecure and as inadequate as you do. When I face those situations, I ask myself: what would be the worst that could happen? If I get ridiculed, or laughed at, what would happen? Is my desire to express and follow my convictions stronger than that fear? Do I believe in my message and the benefits it will bring to others?

Understanding my own feelings towards approaching people, made me realise something curious: When I focused my attention on myself and what I wanted to get, I felt more nervous and afraid. But when I focused my attention on the people and started seeing them as what they are: Normal people with feelings, needs and wishes just like I am, then my conversations with them became much more fluid, more natural and thus the experiences were more positive overall.

When we don't pay too much attention to ourselves, and shift the attention to others, your ego has no time to self-judge. You give him no time and no power to think too much about what you are doing. You are granting at the same time, a great level of attention and interest to the others, and automatically those will feel more sympathetic to you, which will create a positive environment and will reinforce your mental peace. For example, if you are in a job interview and feel very nervous speaking about yourself, you could shift the situation and show a genuine interest in the interviewers and ask them as well many questions related to the job, the company or even personal and listen attentively; that will create an atmosphere of equality and will automatically erase the tension on the air so common in such experiences.

Dale Carnegie, a famous American writer and lecturer in topics of self-development, proposes in his book, *How to win friends and influence people*, multiple principles that will help you in getting better relationships with people, which will result as well in a decrease of fear in dealing with others. I will share my personal favourites with you in a nutshell, but I fully recommend to get Dale's book if you want to deep dive into the topic:

Show genuine interest in others: One of the key secrets of success in dealing with others is the ability to get the other people's point of view and develop the capability to see things from that person's angle. You can learn this by having an honest interest about what and how other

110

people communicate to you and focus on what interests them and how can you help them in getting what they want.

Smile: One big generous smile says more than a full speech of good-intentioned rubbish. Hasn't it happened to you that when someone smiles at you, you automatically like the person, even without exchanging any single word? I bet so!

Like Dale Carnegie says: *"Actions speak louder than words, and a big smile says - I like you, you make me happy, I am glad to see you"*.

Remember people's names at all times: Saying a person's name works like magic. When someone mentions your name, it has a resonance in your body and in your mind. It's like a recognition, that someone is acknowledging you as a unique individual, and not just as a number, or as an object to take advantage of. This is one of the first techniques that not only leaders of big corporations and politicians have to master if they want to get enough following; but also anybody who wants to master the art of dealing with people in general.

It's a very simple, common sense thing to do; yet, many people still struggle to remember people's names after the very first introduction. Make it a habit to learn every single name of every person that you deal with in your daily life. This small effort will definitely pay off!

Become an active listener: If you want to overcome the fear of approaching people, one of the best skills to develop is to become a good conversationalist. A good conversationalist is curious by nature. Is a person that listens without interrupting and asks questions that show interest in what the other people is saying. To be interesting, be interested! Ask people about their accomplishments and other topics that you detect they will have joy in answering.

Become interested in what other people care about: Avoid the me, myself and I syndrome. When you approach someone, make a conscious effort to focus your conversations around what the other person is interested in talking about. In that way, if you focus first on the person's interest, then by the time you have to talk about your request, the environment of the conversation will be more inviting, more positive and more open. The probability that the person will respond positively to your request will increase significantly.

Be sincere in your appreciation to others: Almost every person you meet considers himself or herself very important. If you reinforce that feeling of importance by shifting your attention in remarking their importance, they will like you instantly. However, this approach needs to be sincere. You have to recognise authentically the importance of the other person and articulate it in a way that resonates the most with them.

"Talk to people about themselves and they will listen for hours."

- Benjamin Disraeli, ex British Prime Minister.

The truth is that other people want to feel special. They want to feel accepted and have their value recognised. If you invest your energy there, you will not have to worry about your own 'performance'. People will be so busy talking about themselves and their needs, that after having a conversation with you they will have a good feeling about it and think highly of you. If you approach a big audience, the same applies. Direct your speech to them. Engage them in the conversation. Display examples and cases that resonate with them. Do not spend the whole time talking about you. It's never about you nobody cares about you!

Fear of not being recognised will take another angle the moment you shift your attention to the others. Paradoxically, shifting the attention away from you will have a contrary effect; the more you give your attention to others, the more the others will pay attention to you, and the more highly regarded you will be. It's a great thing to try, isn't it?

Reconnecting back with yourself: Speak your truth

More often than not, our source of fear comes from a feeling of inadequacy. You feel inadequate because you are not sure about what you feel, what you believe and why you act in a certain way. This behaviour is a consequence of not knowing yourself well. If your basic foundations are unknown to you, it is possible that you behave erratically in different situations, according to what you believe 'fits best' with the situation, or what are the feelings of the moment.

To know your truth is to have a very good awareness of who you are. What motivates you to think, and act in a certain way?

People who do not understand themselves, tend to get more anxious and scared, because they put all their worth and praise in elements of their life that they cannot control. They are not true to themselves because, how can they be if they don't know who they are? They like one thing for a time when is trendy and then they shift to the next thing. They are faithful to people temporarily - only when it fits to their blissful interest of the moment. People with no vision, no understanding of their values, and who don't have really a plan for their lives, are more prone to be afraid and anxious at what life 'throws' at them and are more likely to experience more fear of failure- and eventually get more failure- than the ones that know themselves, and know what they are after. A failure does not deviate them from their vision, because they have the certainty that their life is worthwhile pursuing, and so the setbacks are just part of the rich life experience they envision.

That's why all the work done on the first pillars described in the previous sections of this book are so fundamental, because they guide you and push you to make enough self-introspection to help you discover the truth about yourself: *Who am I? What is the plan for my life? What do I have to do to get there? What is important for me?*

When you know yourself, you speak your truth. When you think, act and speak from your truth, failure does not represent a big threat anymore. The coherence of your existence is so clear that the only natural way to act will be on the direction to your vision, in the present moment. The rest will be secondary.

"Is not the critic who counts, not the man who points out how the strong man stumbles, or where the doer of deeds could have done them better.

The credit belongs to the man who is actually on the arena, whose face is marred by dust and sweat and blood; who strives valiantly; who errs, who comes short again and again,

because there is no effort without error and shortcoming; but who does actually strive to do the deeds; who knows great enthusiasm, the great devotions; who spends himself in a worthy cause;

who at the best knows in the end the triumph of high achievement, and who at the worst, if he fails, at least fails while daring greatly ..."

- Theodore Roosevelt

#TheKnechtWay to overcome the fear of failure

- Fear, in scientific terms is an emotion triggered by a biochemical reaction manifesting the perception of danger; it can be a real danger (from the environment) or an imaginary one (coming from the thought process);

- Fear in the metaphysical sense of the human psyche, is the result of a complete disconnection from the present moment and the inner Self.

- A disconnection from the present make us feel vulnerable: Vulnerability or powerlessness is a feeling of incapability about how to approach uncertain situations.

- The best way to overcome fear once you are already experiencing it, is by reassessing his weight of importance: What is the reward if I would act despite my fear? What would be the price to pay if I don't do what I wanted because I was afraid? What has more value to me?

- Most of our fear nowadays come from the need to interact with many people from different backgrounds and cultures. Learning how to interact effectively with people reduces fear and anxiety.

- When having to speak with someone or a wider public, turn your attention to them instead of to you; Focus on what they want and need to hear, and forget about you.

- Speak your truth. When you talk from a deep certainty of who you are and what is your truth, the anxiety and fear of dealing with things in life will be less intimidating.

I have prepared a bonus exercise in the booklet that you can download in the Success Mindset webpage, which will help you in developing strategies for increasing your mental strength when dealing with stressful or fearful situations. Check it out!

Questions for Reflection:

1. *List five things or situations you fear the most*

2. *What is exactly what makes you feel afraid from those things or situations?*

3. *What can you change in yourself to help you deal better with those situations?*

4. *What would be the worst thing that could happen?*

5. *What would you do, if you wouldn't be afraid?*

6. *What elements of your fear could you use to your advantage?*

7. *If you feel afraid of people's reactions to your words and actions, how could you approach people differently so that you can win them over?*

"Speak your truth. When you talk from a deep certainty of who you are and what is your truth, the anxiety and fear of dealing with things in life will be less intimidating."

Paola Knecht

Sixth Pillar

Master your Focus and Self-discipline

*G*ary Player is one of the most successful golfers of all time and is considered a legend in this discipline. He has won nine consecutive world championships during his career until present time. In a recent interview, he revealed what it was that made him a champion in his art at such a young age:

Interviewer: "How did it feel to reach the very top of your sport and become a legend?"

Gary Player: "It was very satisfying because becoming the best golfer in the world was a goal I set as a young boy. Getting to where I am today was extremely difficult and took unbelievable sacrifice and hard work."

Interviewer: "A few shots on the range and a quick jog round the block?"

Gary Player: "No, no, no, no! I did something that no athlete had ever done. I went through the torture cell. My mother died when I was eight, and my father worked eight thousand feet down the mine. My brother went to war at seventeen to fight with the British, while my sister went to boarding school. I'd come all the way home from school each night, by bus and tram, to a dark house, nobody there. I was eight. I've got to cook my food, iron my clothes, get up in the morning at five. I lay in bed every night wishing I was dead, crying.

It's the reason I became a champion: because I knew what it was to suffer. To struggle. And to never give up".

I'm curious. What do you think after reading this small part of Gary's story? My takeaway is that despite the tremendous amount of suffering he experienced as a child, he still kept focused and worked incessantly towards what he wanted. He found his vision at a young age. No success would have been possible if he didn't keep an extraordinary amount of focus and discipline. Gary always worked harder and harder. He always practiced his golf swings, day and night while the others were watching TV. He knew where he wanted to be and worked, worked and worked until he got there. His motto is "The harder I work, the luckier I get".

When you have a clear vision, set your goals aligned with your core values, and you surrender to the present, your intuition will serve you as a GPS. It will show you every step along the way. All you have to do is to remain focused on your vision, and your intuition (GPS) will guide you in the right direction.

Being focused means to pay particular attention to something. In order for us to pay attention, we need to stay truly present in the moment; to *throw yourself* into the activity you are doing without distractions. It sounds easy, but actually, staying focused requires you to be disciplined and concentrated on the moment.

How many times have you gone through your day completely conscious of all your activities, thoughts and actions? How many of those twenty-four hours of the day, were spent in something that was significant for you? And how many of those hours have been just wasted in things that are taking you nowhere?

Although it's still a mystery how our mind brings into consciousness the object of attention, it's well known in the scientific arena that the brain has the ability to concentrate its faculties in just a handful of experiences, enough to keep you alive. The cerebral cortex, which is the outer layer of the cerebral hemisphere, is the responsible of performing and regulating all the complex functions of thought, memory, reasoning, consciousness and attention. We receive billions of bits of information every day at every moment, so our brain cortex has the task to sort out what is relevant out of those tons of information and then decode, process and convert it into something useful.

If we don't participate actively and consciously in the thought process (we let the cerebral cortex function alone present to us what is relevant) the brain will always come up with something it already pre-learned that has worked in the past, which will bring the same results and the same thought patterns. To recalibrate your focus, you need to bring into conscious attention the object of focus, and then have the ability to keep the concentration on it for a prolonged amount of time.

The classic example of how it works is when someone tells you not to think of a yellow car. The first thing the brain will do is guess what? Project the image of a yellow car. You will start to see it everywhere. Why? Because by decoding this information you consciously gave an instruction to the cerebral cortex to focus the attention on the yellow car, by reinforcing in your reason not to think about it. The brain will first visualise the first command before it can follow the second. In the practice of logotherapy this is a common technique called paradoxical intention[2].

---

[2] For more information about paradoxical intention, check Frank Viktor, *In Search of a Meaning* in the reference section.

You can use the paradoxical intention in your favour by bringing into focus the object, activity or thought you want to focus on, and your cerebral cortex will deliver it efficiently to you.

To be focused is basically to set priorities in your daily life. To be observant and plan your day in a way that you do only what is needed for the fulfilment of your vision and what is really important for you.

Do you ever wonder why you never have enough time to do all the activities that you plan to do during the day? It seems like if you want to fit all your priorities in a schedule, it simply ends up in disaster because you do not even reach the half before the day is already ending. If that happens often to you, you might want to re-think about what you are classifying as priority. We often have a long list of things to do. Some are urgent and important, others are just urgent, and some others just important. Which ones do you attend first?

Being efficient does not mean that you have to do all the activities on your list. Being efficient and focused on what matters, is about thinking which resources you can use to optimise the results, as well as which topics you chose to work on first. If you only attend what is urgent, then you end up working the whole day on what is urgent which might be things that are a temporary solution to a bigger problem, and leave behind what would be really important. Obviously, what is urgent and important should get priority, but do not underestimate what is important and not urgent. Those tend to be the kind of activities that look for long term results, and if we ignore them, we may end up getting no results at all.

In our daily lives, we tend to focus on the urgent only. That's why some people do not see real results, despite the big amount of work they do every day. Remember that work alone is leading you nowhere; but work with a specific intention takes you somewhere. If you redirect your actions in the direction you want, you are making the best use of your focusing powers.

Focus is one of the key ingredients to go from where you are, to where you want to be. I believe that the art of focusing is basically letting the creative energy flow through you in a diligent way, fueling its powers into the activity you are doing at the moment. So far in this section, we have learned that focus is paramount to perform any action successfully. Now, you might be wondering where does self-discipline fits in all of this? I believe both are deeply interconnected. If your life would be an automobile, focus is what maintains and optimises the fuel (passion) and the discipline is what keeps the automobile moving.

The amount of focus and discipline you apply to your life goals are bigger indicators of success than talent alone. As Thomas Edison once said, *"Talent is 1% inspiration and 99% perspiration"*. All the work done in identifying your vision and connecting your passion is part of the 1% of the job. Success will come if you are willing to go through the 99% of the hard work.

Every great achievement started with the seed of self-discipline

Self-discipline will be the vehicle in which your priorities will materialise and transform into the path that takes you to your vision.

It's not a secret. Self-discipline takes patience and courage. Most of us do not like to work very hard. We expect that life should happen exactly the way we want it, with not much effort from our side. That's why most of the people remain average. When I say average, I mean, they aim at little and stay with little. They are afraid to dream big, not only because they don't think they can accomplish it, but also because they know that going after a big dream will mean hard work, sacrifice and getting out of the comfort zone.

That's why our culture today loves movie stars, football sensations, business gurus, self-made millionaires and people of the sort that promise the good easy life. They seem like they accomplish everything so easily; from the outside it seems like they didn't have to do much to accomplish their position. We think, that person got really lucky, and was already born talented, so it was a matter of good luck. But as we already learned, the reality is far from what we see on the surface.

Swiss tennis legend Roger Federer, considered the best tennis player in history, is another living example of this truth. He has mentioned in numerous occasions that self-discipline and endless endurance trainings were the key to his success. From one of his famous quotes: "There is no way around hard work. Embrace it. You have to put in the hours because there is always something which you can improve".

American tennis star Serena Williams is another featured example of how maintaining a strong discipline can be the main enabler to achieve all your dreams. Besides being one of the best tennis female players of all times, she is a mother, an entrepreneur, a philanthropist, a fashion icon and even performed several acting roles in movies and TV series. With such a multifaceted and busy schedule, Serena likes to keep her priorities straight by using time management tools, like using apps where she can write down every single minute of her schedule, to see where and how she is spending most of her precious time.

The achievement of great things in life can only be possible when you develop a strong commitment to yourself and believe firmly in your cause. It is the moment when hard work directed towards your intentions becomes the powerful vehicle to achieve all you want in life.

ACTION:

How disciplined are you?

Commit yourself to a goal that has been around your mind but you hadn't fulfilled it yet. It can be something simple like committing to go out for a jog two times a week for thirty minutes. Start with something small and when you reach the goal, go into something bigger! Share with me your experience. Was it hard to stick to it? If yes, what got in the way?

Write me your thoughts on Instagram using the hashtag #Success-WithKnecht

Key elements of self-discipline

"If you want to master the mind and remove your governor, you will have to become addicted to hard work. Because passion and obsession, even talent are only useful tools if you have the work ethic to back them up."

- David Goggins

So what does it take to build a strong self-discipline?

Determination: It is a mixture of passion and perseverance which keeps us moving forward despite the obstacles.

Practice: Repetition of simple activities, during a certain period of time can transform the ordinary to the extraordinary. The greatest abilities which are performed with great precision, are the ones that are executed in the most rigorous and corrected ways.

"We have to develop the instinct of what one can achieve through their greatest efforts."

- Albert Einstein

Resilient mentality: We will fail. There will be days that we would like to just give up because we don't see results after many attempts. Having a resilient mentality will help us overcome those bad moments. Resilience means remaining positive and calm even in the worst of the events. If we remain positive and hopeful, even if things don't work out as planned, will keep us on the game. We will talk more about resilience in the ninth pillar.

Stay alert: The fact that we are focused performing certain actions restlessly should not blind us from the 'whole'. It's important to keep ourselves alert of any activity that is not really serving us so that we can change it.

Flexibility: In this world change is the only constant. There will be points in our lives where external situations will change completely our plans. One important element of being disciplined is the ability to remain flexible and make changes accordingly. It is our responsibility to adapt to new circumstances to avoid getting stuck in doing things that do not work anymore in the present situations.

A focused approach to problem-solving

We admire leaders because we believe that they have a great ability not only to inspire people, but also an outstanding capability to solve problems. The ability and discipline to solve problems is the number one asset that most people get paid for. In my long quest researching and studying successful leaders, I became also particularly interested in understanding what is their approach regarding problem-solving. Big leaders face and solve big challenges, so I became very curious about finding out what was the magic formula they possessed so I could also test it in my own life and share it with others.

My findings, surprisingly, have led almost always to the same basic approach when it comes to problem-solving. Whether that person was a businessman, an athlete, a politician, a writer or an artist, they basically followed the same methodology that I am about to share with you shortly.

Are you ready to find out?

It turns out, the mysterious art of problem-solving can be tackled in a few simple steps:

1. When you are confronted with a difficult problem, start thinking what is good about the existing situation. Do not focus on the bad parts, only on the good ones!

2. Then start to imagine different scenarios in which the situation can be better. How would things look better?

3. Start generating as many ideas as you can for how you could improve the current situation.

4. Write down all the ideas. Do not judge them yet, just write them. Simply write all that comes to your mind.

5. Re-evaluate the ideas and try to find actions that could support the execution of those ideas.

6. Select three of them and act on them immediately.

The most important thing is to start acting as soon as possible and get focused on the solutions instead of spending too much time trying to understand the problem.

Not a breakthrough finding, isn't it?

One aspect of the methodology that was different from what I have learned towards problem-solving is actually the way you start. Normally, we tend to start paying too much attention trying to understand the problem. I have experienced this especially when working with big companies or large groups of people. We tend to dedicate day long discussions trying to find out what went wrong, why it went wrong, who is there to blame, what was the root cause etc., etc. So, an interesting insight when learning the approach from great leaders, was the fact that they focus more on the 'good' side of the story. The problem is there, we cannot do anything about it, so what's next? What is still good about it? And how can we make the situation better?

Starting from looking at the good side of the situation sets you automatically in a more positive, solution-mode, creative approach, in my view, much better than starting with the negatives of drilling into the problem.

Do not get me wrong. I still believe it's important to understand the root causes of the problems and learn from them so that you avoid repeating the same mistakes in the future. But I believe that we must pay much more attention on the solution and keep moving forward instead of spending too much time digging into the problem. Otherwise, if we spend all our time and energy in the problem, what amount of time and energy will be left for finding the solution?

Remember that indecision, fear and worry, are the main killers of focus and action! And digging too long into the problem will set you in a negativity spiral which will be hard to get out of.

In the end, the ultimate winner is the person that has the focus and the discipline to work on their goals and dreams, approaching and solving obstacles as they go, every single day.

How to become a master in self-discipline

The topic of self-discipline fascinates me. I feel astonished to see how a human being can transform himself/herself into something completely different by only being disciplined in their approach. It's a wonderful metamorphosis. Self-discipline for me is that mysterious inner work; I relate it metaphorically with the pupa, the stage in between when the caterpillar becomes a beautiful butterfly. Nobody, not even scientists really understand what is going on inside of the pupa. They know what comes after, which is the beautiful butterfly, but what are the mechanisms that allow that transformation to happen?

It's a plain black mystery. As it is what happens to our brains and our hearts when we commit to go through our metamorphosis via self-discipline.

The word 'discipline' comes from the Latin *discipulus*, which means student learner or follower. From *discipulus* comes *disciplina* which in Latin means instruction and knowledge. Therefore, self-discipline means being a 'self-learner' and a 'self-follower'. In short, you self-learn from the master, which is you.

To have self-discipline, is one of the truest acts of self-love. You regard yourself as your own disciple, which will follow and do what is needed to keep self-learning; and the more you know about yourself, the more you are in a position to feel empowered and confident to do whatever you want in life.

I could give you an interminable list of suggestions how to master your self-discipline. But let's be honest here. If you expect a list of magic tricks to suddenly get the virtue of discipline, then you better look in another book. I will tell you the harsh truth.

You want to hear it? I guess you want to.

No expert, no doctor, no guru, no leader, no one, can tell you how to build *your* own self-discipline.

This was my honest finding when I was researching this topic. I always hoped to find the magic technique, the all-mighty, the secret hidden key of all the overachievers of the world. I looked restlessly at as much of the literature and biographies I could get just to find out that the only thing that separates the disciplined person from the undisciplined is the following: *Faith.*

Faith in oneself is the only thing that you need. You see, you can set any goal you wish, easy or difficult. You can write a plan how to achieve it. You can get yourself into action. But after a certain amount of time, that initial motivation and internal drive, all that can fade away as soon as you are confronted with the first hardships. Plans can change, things can fail, and the whole world can turn upside down. Your emotions going along with all those changes. So, what is the original seed, the only thing that remains stable, even if the whole thing falls apart?

That's right, your faith.

Last, unwavering faith in yourself.

No matter what will happen, or how it will happen, you will never give up in yourself because you have faith in yourself.

And so, discipline is a by-product of having faith. Faith is what keeps running the inner work in the mysterious paths of our minds and our hearts, so that we keep growing. You might change the methods, the targets, the means, but you will keep your faith unshakable, and as a result, after a period of time, you will suddenly become a whole new person.

A last word about faith worth mentioning. Viktor Frankl, an Austrian neurologist, psychiatrist and philosopher who survived the concentration camps during the Second World War, went as far as to say that what keeps us alive, is our intrinsic relationship between our emotional state, our degree of faith and its repercussions in our immunological system. Basically, what he says is that when you keep a strong faith associated with an intense emotional state, you can survive even extreme experiences like life-death situations.

In his own words: "Those who know the strong relationship between the emotional state of a person - her values and her hope, or the lack thereof - and the functioning of her immunological system will understand that the sudden loss of faith can culminate in death".

This is a powerful take away: the same fuel that keep us alive in times of crisis, which is *faith*, is the one that can sustain our self-discipline!

#TheKnechtWay to develop extraordinary focus and self-discipline

- Focus and self-discipline are indispensable allies for reaching anything in life worth pursuing.
- The art of focus is the capability to maintain the attention span of a particular activity during an uninterrupted amount of time.
- Focus is the channel where creative energy is concentrated.
- Self-discipline is the act of doing a certain activity consistently over long periods of time.
- Self-discipline takes patience and courage.
- Practice, resilience, alertness and flexibility are the key elements to build a strong self-discipline.
- Problem-solving is an important aspect of self-discipline. Your capability to solve problems will set you apart from others.
- Behind the art of strong self-discipline and focus is the unwavering, strong faith in oneself and in the things that you can accomplish.

Questions for Reflection

1. *Think about three things you want to get done today. How can you focus your attention to help you get them done?*

2. *Think about something you really want to achieve this month. What motivates you to do it? What will be the outcome if you make it happen?*

3. *List ten things you compromise yourself to do this month to improve your focus and self-discipline*

4. *Do you have faith in yourself? What would change in your motivation and in your level of energy if you knew that all you want in life can be and will be accomplished?*

"Discipline is a by-product of having faith. Faith is what keeps running the inner work in the mysterious paths of our minds and our hearts, so that we keep growing. You might change the methods, the targets, the means, but you will keep your faith unshakable, and as a result, after a period of time, you will suddenly become a whole new person."

Paola Knecht

Seventh Pillar

Create a Winning Self-Image

*W*hat if I tell you that you are not who you think you are?

Maybe you will roll your eyes at me and say that I'm crazy. What nonsense are you saying?

You would probably argue back telling me you *do know* who you are. You will tell me your name, your profession, your background, the city where you were born, your interests, your successes and failures lots of stories.

The construction of yourself, who you believe you are, started since the early memories of your childhood all the way up to now. You have gathered all these years, a lot of information that give you an estimation of the person you believe you are: What your parents, teachers, friends, partners and society have told you. Based on their judgements and your own validation of their judgements, you have self-created a character, which you claim to be yourself.

When you wake up in the morning, what do you decide to wear? What are the thoughts that came through you while getting ready? How do you organise your morning, what do you eat for breakfast and how you go on with your day? All these things are telling you which self-image you have chosen for yourself and that image is what you also project to the world.

Dr Maxwell Maltz, author of one of the most popular books on self-image, *Psycho-Cybernetics*, says that one of the most important psychological discoveries in this last century is the discovery of the 'self-image' which is like a mental blueprint or picture of ourselves; a group of values and beliefs a person has about '*which kind of person I am*'. This image is mainly unconsciously built, and it is the result of all the past experiences, successes and failures, opinions, and emotionally attached circumstances that governed our lives up to now.

But guess what? In reality, everything that you believe you are, are just perceptions thoughts stored in a collective pot in the thin air. Simple and plain, chosen, limited perceptions of a much wider reality.

From the evolutionary theory perspective, it is known by science and psychology that we carry within ourselves certain behavioural traits from our ancestors, which have evolved based on the challenges of the environment and their conscious choices to overcome those challenges. For example, one of the most fascinating results from our organic evolution has been our ability to develop language and adapt it to our specific environment. Karl Popper and John Eccles mention in their book, *The Self and its Brain* that our conscious decision to speak and to take interest in speech, has been one of the reasons why we consciously decided to evolve our minds and brains and that this, "exerted the selection pressure under which emerged the human brain and the consciousness of Self".

We also know that we inherited from our ancestors, certain behavioural traits that have been useful for them in coping with their environment from thousands of generations. As a mother of two small kids, I have learned by first-hand experience something fascinating: We are born with an intuitive knowledge, with certain values and attitudes that I have observed in the behaviour of my own kids. For example, my three-year-old daughter has an innate interest for all living creatures and sees them with love. Every time she sees a creature (i.e. insect, cat, dog or an elephant), she displays a natural attention and care towards them. I am also surprised how she approaches them without any sort of fear; her level of trust in other living entities is pure. My fourteen-month son does not understand the meaning of 'fear or limit'. If he wants something, perhaps to reach a toy from a high table, he tries incessantly to reach it; first he tries to climb; after several attempts (and some injuries), he tries from another angle. If it doesn't work, he will try the next day, and the next until he manages to reach it.

It never ceases to amaze me their curiosity towards life; to see how joyful they are with small things; with the simple act of discovering the world around them. Those innate behaviours which I believe are our intrinsic intuitive knowledge, are most observable with children. Children live in the present, display their spontaneity of being. Unfortunately, this intuitive knowledge is later disowned, for the sake of fitting in our modern 'social construct'.

However, what we should not forget is that from the moment we are born, until this precise moment, we are exposed to a vast array of potentialities of being, from where we have the freedom to choose what to believe, what to think and how to act in any given time.

If you awaken to this fact, you will realise that you *always* have the power to create and mould your self-image at any moment, which is what this seventh pillar is all about: To create a winning self-image that supports your wildest desires. Create and be that person that you wish to be. Make it a reality. Bring it to life!

Viktor Frankl said that one of the highest faculties of man is the capability to decide how his existence will be. From his own words: "Man has the capability to determine himself, does not only limits himself to existence, but he decides how his existence will be, what will it convert to every minute".

Find the Inner You

"Expressing our uniqueness is a revolution that will change every-thing. "

- David Icke

We tend to look at ourselves only through the mirror of the physical world, but we often forget that our existence goes beyond what we call the "physical reality", or the world of matter. All of us know at one degree or another, that there is *something* else that constitutes our existence.

What we know for sure is that we have a body, which has a brain, and part of the functioning features of the brain is to reproduce what we call our mind, and our intellect. We also are aware of the driving metaphysical energy called *consciousness,* which is a life force energy which all living things possess and that we understand very little about how it really works. We only know that without consciousness, there is no perception of life.

Grasping the idea of consciousness as the universal life force will eventually take us to a much wider reality of how to make sense of the world and about who we really are.

Arthur Schopenhauer, a German philosopher, proposed in his main work *The World at Will and his Representation* that our consciousness is the metaphysical form of the *will to live*, which passes through the

138

world as idea, in order to materialise its will through the intellect. Basically, what Schopenhauer calls the *will to live,* is the universal force that inhabits in everything living, so it is essentially an energy that can take any particular form (i.e. a human, a flower, an animal) to express its will.

When we say that the world is all interconnected, that we are all one single living entity, we are affirming that behind what we tend to classify as the environment, the animals and the people, the same metaphysical life forces are governing; so, you as a particular person, are a unique manifestation; a unique point of attention of the universal consciousness being represented in human form.

I don't know about you, but the more I grasp this universal truth the more liberating it feels. What we call 'human personalities' is nothing more than creations from our own making and as such, we have the power to modify them at any time. We have an unlimited source of energy of life wisdom coming and acting through us, and with that comes a vast array of possibilities to shape our existence! Isn't that beautiful?

When we realise who we really are, we understand in a deeper degree that many possibilities are open. You have the power right now to redefine yourself. You do not need to accept the past, nor accept everything that you have believed about yourself or what others think. At any moment, you have the capability to *decide on the person you want to become.*

"The knowledge of image-making eliminates competition from your life by moving you from the competitive plane to the creative plane. You will soon understand therefore, that in truth, the only competition you will ever have is with your own ignorance."

- Bob Proctor

I know all this sounds beautiful and it really is beautiful, but as everything worthwhile pursuing, it comes with its fair share of difficulty. Our old, well established self-image is something we defend a lot. Somehow, we think that without the built image we have about ourselves, we lose our identity- we do not know who we are anymore. As humans, we like to be recognised. We like to belong somewhere, to have an identity. And all we know is what we have experienced so far in life: Our childhood, our life experiences, our thoughts. Without this belonging to us, we feel naked, vulnerable, we feel like we do not really exist.

Please don't get me wrong. I am not suggesting that you have to destroy and delete all your experiences and build everything brand new in your mind. Don't go to the birth register office and change your name and your place of origin just yet! (kidding). We have to put everything in the right perspective. There are elements in your life that makes you unique: Your birthplace, the family you were born to, the culture that shaped your persona, the moral, ethical and religious values. Those elements make your life rich and meaningful.

The idea I want to express in relation to modifying your self-image is about detecting those values and beliefs about yourself that are limiting you, that most likely came as a result of a previous experience you had. Is not the experience or the life circumstance *per se* that you have to deny; it is the constructed belief and self-judgement that came as a consequence. We can definitely do not change our past or the present circumstances. But we can change what we make out of them. This is completely in our control.

My question for you at this point would be: Is your current self-image serving you in reaching what you want in life? Are you happy with

140

your self-image? Do you believe that how you see yourself now is all what you can become?

If the answer is yes in all the questions, then you don't need to read this section any further. You nailed it! But if the answer is no to at least one of them, then stay with me, there's more to learn.

Create a self-image that fits to who you want to become

I remember when I was in fourth grade. I used to be afraid of maths. Somehow, I never felt I was good at it. Because my conviction of this fact was so strong, I did not try hard to understand or to get better at it. Then, as a self-fulfilling prophecy, whenever there was a math test I failed or passed with the lowest grade. This belief that I was bad at maths stayed with me for a long time. It became a feature of who I believed I was.

The single act of having to study for a math test was so terrifying that when the time came to actually having to do it, I procrastinated it during the day and just studied the bare minimum at night before going to bed, to get over it. Then one day, after receiving a failing note in one of the most important tests, my math professors told me: "*You really need to look for help. You are not good and I doubt you will ever be*". Something inside me just exploded. I felt angry at the time with my professor, but even more with myself. This apparently simple event made a big click inside of me.

I was tired of being the stupid math student. So, I made the decision to change that. I started to work harder, to pay attention and study seriously. My grades improved. My self-confidence improved. I realised math was not really that difficult if I really pay attention to what I was actually doing. With time, I discovered that I actually loved math; to the point that when the time came to choose a bachelor study, I went for engineering.

This is a story with a happy ending. I finally ended up graduating with honours as an Engineer. This life experience made me learn something very valuable about the beliefs I had about myself, and about how life works: If I had kept my childhood belief that I was bad at math, and accepted the judgment of my professor that '*I was not good and never will be*', I wouldn't have learned that I was actually good at it. My confidence would probably be much lower in my capabilities in general, which would carry with itself unnecessary trouble.

Although I am not really a gifted mathematician, I could demonstrate to myself that with a lot of study, practice and focus, I could actually do very well at it. This discovery made me feel quite confident, that actually, any person could achieve anything they want, by facing their limiting beliefs and go on and just try.

How confidence can boost your self-image

"You must find yourself acceptable to you. You must have a wholesome self-esteem. You must have a self that you can trust and believe in. You must have a self that is not ashamed to 'be' and one that you can feel free to express creatively, rather than hide or cover-up."

- Dr Maxwell Maltz

Confidence and self-image are strongly interrelated concepts. Being confident basically means to '*believe in yourself*'. If you have a positive self-image, you will definitely have more confidence than by having a negative and low self-image.

Most of our perceived confidence in adulthood comes from recalling those accumulated successes that are stored in our minds. A confident person knows that no matter what the circumstances, in the end, he or she will be capable of achieving his or her goal. It is to have faith in oneself, and to love oneself to the point that even if the desired goal is not achieved in the first try, there is a certainty that eventually it will

143

come to pass, as long as one keeps trying. We must also remember that real confidence, which comes from self-acceptance, is a trait that is already inherent in our 'Self. Kids love and accept themselves in their early childhood years.

Even though confidence is part of our inner nature, for most people, confidence has a weak foundation, because it is built on external opinions that have been interiorised and considered as theirs, without really listening to their own real voice. Dr Maxwell Maltz mentions in his book, *Psycho Cybernetics* that all humans possess a success servo mechanism, which is basically responsible for keeping us alive. All the creatures in this world have been preset for succeeding at living; however, we as humans are longing for more than just our pure survival: We have as well many emotional and spiritual needs, that also need to be fulfiled in order to feel self-realised.

If you follow your inner compass, also called your internal voice, you can discover your personality. That personality comes out as the external evidence of your real individual and creative self. A personality that emerges from the heart is unique and precious. It's magnetic and attractive, because it comes from the source of the divine. When you are aware of your real personality, you are no longer afraid to act, in fact, you act spontaneously, because there is something inside of you that reconfirms that no matter what happens, the need to preserve your true nature is stronger than anything else.

People with 'poor personality' or 'no personality', are the ones that block their real Self due to fear: Fear to express himself, fear of the opinions of others, of not being liked, of being ashamed and being hurt.

You can easily recognise people that have a good personality: They are energetic, positive, attractive; Full of life. People with poor personalities are shy, too self-conscious, rigid and lack creativity and poise.

It's worthwhile to take a moment here to observe your own personality. What is your opinion of it? Do you like it? Do you enjoy being with yourself?

If you feel at ease; if you enjoy your own company above all, and you feel relaxed and in peace most of the time, my sincere Congratulations; you are one of those rare people that are able to manifest their inborn, wonderful and attractive persona.

On the other side, if you feel misplaced, inconvenient, anxious or even angry with yourself; then you need to pull all the breaks and observe what is going on. What are those illusionary beliefs that are attacking you, and not letting your own light shine? What can you do to regain the inborn and pure self-confidence that already sits within you? Recall the fact that you have the power to change your self-image at any moment. As we have been reviewing throughout the book, you know that with enough will, discipline and faith in yourself you can regain it back!

"So attend carefully to your posture. Quit drooping and hunching around. Speak your mind. Put your desires forward, as if you had a right to them—at least the same right as others. Walk tall and gaze forthrightly ahead. Dare to be dangerous. Encourage the serotonin to flow plentifully through the neural pathways desperate for its calming influence."

- Jordan Peterson

The key to have a good, positive, adequate and creative personality is to have a healthy confidence. Too much self-confidence leads to arrogance and it can cause a disruptive view about yourself, which will at the end cause you more trouble than good.

BONUS: What other ingredients make the 'success-type' personality? Check out the free booklet on the book's webpage to access extra information and tips in how to create a self-image that is set for success.

Signs of Overconfidence

Let's say, you are one of those that have a high level of self-confidence. Great! But how could you find out if you are crossing the line and being overconfident?

An overconfident person:

- Gets into a lot of trouble every time she expresses her opinion

- Perform irrational actions without considering the opinions of others

- Has a big issue in admitting that she is wrong

- Often finds himself in difficult situations because he 'spoke too fast'

- Does not take into account opinions of others

- Has a strong need to always be right

If you identify yourself with some features in this list, try to become more conscious of your actions and make an effort to keep an open mind about things. A good personality has a good balance between overconfidence and a lack of it. When you feel adequate with yourself, you will experience a more calm, creative and energetic space where you can better express yourself.

Overconfidence can be dangerous. If you are too reliant on your capabilities, you can also lose the opportunity to enhance connection with others which builds creativity.

The other side of the coin: lack of confidence

Lack of confidence is the number one reason why people don't go after their dreams.

When we were little kids, we learnt that we have to follow what others expected from us. Our parents expected total obedience to their demands. Our teachers pretty much the same. If we did everything that they wanted, we got rewarded. If not, we got punished. This constant suppression makes us forget our true spontaneous nature of being.

Over time, we learn that what makes you successful is to fulfil other people's demands. We grow far away from listening to our own demands and so we end up at one point in our lives feeling frustrated because we do not recognise ourselves anymore.

Although it's important to build good relationships with people, that doesn't mean that we have to surrender to all their demands. Hey, it's actually good and healthy sometimes to be disliked and follow your own desires. In fact, there is a famous philosophy developed by the German psychiatrist Alfred Adler, which is called Adlerian Psychology which supports this fact.

Some of the most prominent ideas from his theory of individual psychology can be summarised as:

Free will dominate over determinism: What happens to you right now is unrelated to your past or to the present circumstances; the reality is that *you chose to feel and act in a certain way* and you are using your past or the current situation to justify your behaviour and telling to yourself that nothing can be changed. Adler believes it is people who fabricate their own anger and create their own trauma, by deliberately choosing to do so. However, you can change your behaviour and actions at any moment. You have the free will to do it. The only person that stops you is yourself.

All problems are interpersonal problems: Adler reinforces in his theory the fact that all our problems are collective, self-made constructs in our own minds. The real root of our problems are coming from inferiority complexes, which are all subjective assumptions created by ourselves. We cannot control what other people think or do, so why worry about it? The moment we stop seeing interpersonal relationships as competition, we will experience the real joy of collaboration and self- acceptance.

Another interesting point is about how to separate your 'life tasks' with 'other people's tasks'. Authors Kishimi and Koga in their book, *The Courage to be Disliked* which is based in the Adlerian Psychology, say that "In general, all interpersonal relationship troubles are caused by intruding in other people's tasks or having one's own tasks intruded on". I found this statement fascinating, because it is so simple and yet so powerful. By having the capability to separate our tasks, we could make big changes in our life.

Let's put an example about how to do it. If you are a parent, you worry that your kids go to school and do their homework. If one of our kids refuse to go to school or do any homework, what is what we as parents usually do? That's right we try to force them to do what we want. We interfere in their task which is to study and go to school. But who has the real responsibility of studying and going to school? The parents or the kids? Your role as a parent is to be a guiding force; by letting the kids choose by themselves what to do and bear their own results. The kid's task is to study and go to school.

148

How many times did you get angry at people that *'messes up with your stuff'*? Parents, teachers or peers taking decisions on your behalf? How many times you took responsibilities that were not really your own? For example, you took the guilt, the 'feeling sorry for', kind of behaviour?

The art of separating your own tasks with other's tasks and also discard people's tasks that are not your responsibility, is something we have to master in order to make our life simpler. Like Kishimi and Koga say: *"All you can do with regards to your own life is choose the best path you believe in. On the other hand, what kind of judgement do other people pass on that choice? That's the task of other people, and it doesn't matter because you cannot do anything about it"*.

Contribution to others: In essence, Adler believed that people who are overly concerned about themselves miss the opportunity to contribute to society in a meaningful way. You can contribute by thinking more of others instead of yourself when you perform your tasks and see others as 'comrades' instead of 'enemies'. To have unconditional trust in others, is the ultimate effect of self-acceptance.

On the other hand, doing something in particular doesn't necessarily add value to your life; Just by being is enough. Think of the value of a newborn baby. The baby cannot 'compete' in the rat race of work and money. The baby just exists and his existence brings the highest of joys to their parents and family.

Life is a portrait of moments: My favourite point from Adler's: Life is what is happening now. Life is like a dance; you delight yourself swinging, twisting, and trying new movements as you move along. Life shouldn't be about moving from A to B in the most efficient way possible; if that would be the case, why bother to live? If you travel to Paris with the only purpose to see the Eiffel tower, why to bother to sit in the cafés, walk around the park, try the delicious croissants, and visit the Louvre? That would be inefficient.

Life is not about being efficient, it is about living and delighting in your existence.

In a nutshell: to live in order to please others is like living their lives and not yours. The moment you have the courage to stand for your own life, something finally clicks in within yourself. You realise that what you are really in charge of, is to live your own life; that's why you have been granted with one body and mind.

If you want to develop a mindset that is set for your own success, then a lack of confidence cannot be part of your life.

The power of positive thinking

Positive thinking represents one simple thing: Being optimistic about ourselves, about our capabilities, and about life circumstances.

We all come to this world in a helpless state, as fragile creatures. It's in our nature to desire to escape from that helpless state and become 'superior'. We are at any moment in our lives, directly or indirectly looking for ways to improve and to grow. You can see it very clearly in a little child: A toddler inherently wants to pass from crawling to walking. They fall and try again and again until they master it by themselves. You don't have to teach them anything or tell them anything: they automatically look for the way to grow and improve. The inferiority complex comes when we become self-conscious about our desire to be superior, but fall short according to our expectations of progress. If we focus too much in our shortfalls instead of our progresses, we can generate negative patterns of thought.

Negativity reinforces the idea that you are not enough; a negative thought pattern will result in losing faith in yourself, which can throw you in a spiral where you get trapped in a cycle where you get negative thoughts, get anxious, you will not take action or will take the wrong actions, which will lead you to getting the wrong results.

Every time you find yourself thinking negatively, change it immediately for positive thoughts. It will be difficult in the beginning, but with the time, you will develop a positive stamina, which will definitely help you in feeling better, make better decisions and increase overall the confidence and security in yourself.

Some of you might be wondering at this point what do I mean by positive thoughts. What means to think positively?

To think positive, in my experience, is to consciously make an effort to look at things with the lenses of Love and not Fear. Is to be optimistic about the future and confident that no matter what happens, everything will turn alright at the end. Plato, the famous disciple of Socrates, illustrated this state of negativity in human consciousness in his famous cave allegory: Basically, human beings live in ignorance of the truth, similar to prisoners in a cave. These prisoners are sitting facing a wall bound in chains, with the fire between them making shadows on the wall. All the prisoners can see are the shadows, which they believe it's the reality.

Generations come and go, until one prisoner starts to question what is behind the walls of the prison and what's beyond the shadows; he decides to walk towards the end of the cave and discovers a hole in which he can go out of the cave. He discovers a wonderful outside world, full of light and colours. He then returns back to the cave to tell others what he had seen; however, the others refuse to believe him, call him crazy and prefer to keep looking at the shadows of the wall. Something similar we do to our consciousness when we refuse to see the 'other side', the positive side of reality and just stick with pessimistic thoughts about our circumstances.

I saw great changes in my life when I discovered the power of positive thinking. I used to be the kind of person that always worried about the future. I often felt inconvenient or incapable of dealing with situations that I did not know well. I remember when having my first job and I was an amateur, how little I felt in comparison with other colleagues that had a higher, sexier title and had more experience than me. I thought, there is no way that I can match them in intelligence or capability. As you can imagine, those thoughts reflected how I performed in the beginning.

My fear of being perceived as incapable made me act shy, and so I often didn't do more than was requested. I tended to stay on the back and avoided being in the spotlight, doing my work silently; waiting until the end of the working day to go home and complain about my situation. One day however, I have had enough, it was time to get out of the cave. Something in me commanded me to get up and step into the arena. To start raising my voice and my opinion. I had a choice: either to stand up for myself, or let myself be eaten alive in the corporate jungle.

So I decided, every morning, the first thing I was going to do is to demand to myself more respect, more peace of mind, more confidence. I made the conscious commitment to bring to my mind only positive thoughts, like imagining myself excelling at work, developing great relationships with people, and having a great time while working. If something challenging comes my way, I would approach it with an open and curious mind; for example, if there is a situation where I need to respond for a potential delay in a project, or if I have a conflict with a colleague about an important report, instead of taking it personally and getting upset, I ask myself how can I tackle this situation better; what are the alternatives out there? And then focus on looking for a solution that brings the desired result, instead of wasting time blaming myself or others, or thinking too much, which also ends in self-doubt.

The results have been incredible. As soon as I decided to change my thoughts, it was like everything around changed. My boss and colleagues started to treat me with more respect. They acted more collaboratively and were more willing to listen to my suggestions and support them. With this single change in my mental state, I created a whole new world for me. A better world.

Life can be very difficult. We are constantly exposed to the unknown. No one has the power to foresee the future, and nobody has the answers to all questions. We will make mistakes on our way. We will be exposed and feel vulnerable. But the attitude towards how we approach each event is what makes the difference between someone that succeeds and someone that fails. A catastrophe could be seen with two completely different lenses. The person with the negative lenses will succumb and fall in the victim mode. The world will seem unfair and terrible and see himself or herself hopeless. The person with the positive lenses will see it as an opportunity to learn and will find a positive use of the tragedy. It will turn it around for his or her benefit.

Positive thoughts and words do not only affect humanity. Do you know that the words you whisper and the feelings that accompany those words have an effect on all living things and everything around you? If you don't believe me, check out the work from Dr Masaru Emoto. He was a Japanese scientist who discovered through his experiments photographing water molecules with a high-speed camera at their freezing point, that the molecular structures of water changes when they are exposed to human words, thoughts, sounds and intentions.

Water that is exposed to loving and compassionate thoughts and words, result in perfectly shaped, beautiful physical molecular formations in water; whereas ugly, unpleasant thoughts resulted in unpleasant physical molecular formations.

This is a breakthrough discovery which shows that indeed living things are interconnected and we all emit vibrations in different frequency levels, and depending on the frequency is the expression on the physical plane. Positive thoughts have high frequency vibrations which are related to love, kindness, compassion and peace; and create beautiful, perfect shapes. Negative thoughts vibrate in low frequencies where fear, hate, guilt and worry are the dominant feelings and create ugly, erratic shapes. If you want to see more from Mr Emoto's work, I recommend you get his book, *The Hidden Messages of Water*.

154

There have been other experiments carried out which proves the fact that sounds emit a vibrational frequency that forms shapes. Cymatic is the science that studies modal vibrational phenomena in sounds. Erns Chladni, a German musician and physicist discovered in the eighteen century that the modes of vibration of a plate can be seen by sprinkling dust on the surface of a plate connected to an instrument. The oscillations resulting from it made the sand form perfect symmetrical shapes, looking like mandalas. In recent decades, the Swiss physician Hans Jenny published the first book ever released on Cymatics, showing the results of extensive experiments which all demonstrated the effects of sound on fluids, powders and pastes which resulted in ordered, perfect patterns. You can check this extraordinary phenomenon by searching 'Cymatic experiments' on YouTube.

Those amazing proofs should leave you with no doubt about the power of positive thinking, and the power of positive words, thoughts and intentions. A human body is almost seventy percent water; out of it, the brain and heart are seventy-three percent water; and lungs eighty three percent. Even our bones contain thirty one percent of just water! Can you see the repercussion that positive thoughts and words have in the vibrational frequency of your body? I can go as far as to say that positive thoughts are the healing power behind maintaining good mental and physical health.

There's no time to waste in negative thinking!

"To be a positive role-model is the fastest and most powerful way to teach others, because people do not listen to your words with the same profundity to which they feel your actions."

- Mohamed Bin *Rashid Al* Maktoum

#TheKnechtWay to create a winning self-image

You have the power to change your self-image at any moment:

- Understand that you are part of the infinite source of life and you are a unique point of attention of the whole life consciousness, and have a unique mission which must find its most creative expression. That life expression, if found inwardly, will be projected as your personality.

- Cherish your unique life experiences, but change the limited beliefs that keeps you small and is blocking your progress.

- Develop a healthy, adequate, strong and attractive confidence in yourself.

- Be careful not to overrate your confidence; keep a healthy momentum.

- Keep a positive attitude at all times! Positive thoughts are the most beautiful resonance of the cosmos.

Questions for Reflection:

1. *How do you see yourself? Are there aspects from your self-image you would like to change?*

2. *What kind of person you need to become in order to reach the vision you have set for yourself?*

3. *What are the limited beliefs from your current personality that are blocking you from acting in the direction of your goals?*

4. *Observe your thoughts for a moment. Are those thoughts positive or negative? If they are more negative, how can you turn them around?*

5. *What can you do today to help boost your confidence?*

"From the moment we are born, until this precise moment, we are exposed to a vast array of potentialities of being, from where we have the freedom to choose what to believe, what to think and how to act in any given time."

Paola Knecht

Eighth Pillar

Talent alone is not success

"Talent means nothing, while experience, acquired in humility and with hard work, means everything."

– Patrick Süskind

I used to believe that all you needed to be successful in life, was to be born with an extraordinary talent and everybody would recognise it immediately without doing much effort and you will grow wealthy in no time. In some very rare cases it still holds true, but it is not the reality for the majority of us.

Over the years I observed and met people that had great talents, but surprisingly, they did not consider themselves a success; you probably have met them as well. The amazing singer performing at the metro station in exchange for some coins; the gifted and intelligent business colleague that is stuck in a mediocre-paid job; the talented cook that instead of doing her art, is working as an assistant secretary in a large firm. I came across so many people in similar situations that I finally understood that is not really talent what is missing in our human nature; actually, I believe all of us have unlimited gifts and talents that are God given. So, if everybody has a talent, what is the missing trick? Why not everybody is wealthy and successful? Or considers his life complete?

In my quest to find an answer, I studied the lives of several people which I admired and believed were gifted in what they were doing. It surprised me to find out about their humble beginnings and their extraordinary will to make things happen. In any dream they pursued, they kept on moving. They failed. They tried again and again. They learned from their mistakes and kept going. Over time, what was a dream became an enduring passion, which helped them to develop their talent and skill with such an intensity that the only option left was to succeed.

The history of humanity is full of such examples. Judy Blume, an American writer best known for her formidable novel, *God, are you there? It's me, Margaret* started her writing career while being a stay home mom taking care of her two children. Since she was a little kid, she loved to read and write and had a great imagination. However, it was only until attending her first writing courses at NYU university when she began to send several novels to publishers and faced multiple rejections. She focused on writing novels casting teenage girls and exposing the topics of body image and sexuality in the view of a teenager, a topic that was considered taboo in the seventies.

Despite the rejections, criticisms and censorships she had to endure from publishers, it didn't stop her from writing and she became one of the most popular authors for young readers in American history and one of the top leading voices and advocates of intellectual freedom by joining the National Coalition Against Censorship.

Blume has sold more than ninety million copies and her books have been translated to more than thirty-two languages. Her story reminds us about the power of raising your own voice. She believed in herself and in her desire to become an expression for young people whose realities were not represented in American literature at the time. She fought to become their voice through her characters. Her talent as a writer combined with her passion and dedication, were the key ingredients of her outstanding success.

In our modern world, we expect that success happens to us instantly or with little effort.

We see how people post attractive photos and content on Instagram in the hope they become 'viral' just by sharing it with many other people. We believe in magic formulas sold all over the internet, where they promise you to learn a top skill in a matter of minutes and in doing so they sell you a *'shortcut to success'*. Or even worse, they promise to give you a magic formula where all you have to do is invest some money and the rest will take care of itself.

Who has not received such an email: *Earn thousands of dollars by building an email listing without you moving a single finger!* or *Pursue your dream of becoming a best seller author without writing a single page!* It always made me wonder: why would people believe this? That there is a magic formula, a secret moon juice over there just available for people that buy such programs, that you just pay and you will get all your wishes come true – a millionaire, a successful entrepreneur, a bestselling author?

I think what happens in such cases is that we miss the real deal and confuse it with something ephemeral. I like to think of the metaphor used by Schopenhauer when describing the differences between seeing real talent versus something fake: He says there are three types of levels of talent; in his essays he referred specifically to writers, but I think it could be applied to any profession. Basically, there are three types of people: the meteors, the planets, and the fixed stars.

The meteors produce something that is shiny and loud for a brief moment in time; you see it and say "Look! Over there!" And then pum! It vanishes in the sky not to be seen again. I think about all these "instant made" entrepreneurs, influencers and trendy pop singers of the sort would belong to this category. Then you have the planets, that are moving stars that shine sometimes brighter than the fixed stars, when they are closer to them or so it seems but if you really look, they shine on borrowed light, because they do not really generate light on their own.

Here you can have a broader category businesses that last many years, artists with decades of trajectory that are a sensation for one or two generations, but they end up being shadowed and obsolete as soon as the new trends are hitting the new generations. Then, you have the fixed stars, like the sun. They generate their own light and influence all equally regardless of time and space. This kind of talent transcends time, generations, trends, and seem to be atemporal. What comes to my mind here are the great leaders of all times like Nelson Mandela, Martin Luther King, Mahatma Gandhi, religious figures like Christ or Buddha; the great Greek thinkers like Plato, Socrates, Aristoteles; The great scientists like Einstein, and Marie Curie. Their work and influence transcend generation after generation and as Schopenhauer says, "they do not belong to a nation alone; they belong to the Universe".

I like this metaphor a lot because it helps you reflect about what are the levels of transcendence you can aspire to be. Do you want to be a meteor? Or do you want to become a fixed star?

I believe there is nothing wrong in choosing to be a meteor or a planet, as long as you are convinced this is the best for you and you invest an adequate amount of work on it.

If your aspiration is to shoot for the fixed star, then, shortcuts are out of question. There is nothing left but devoting yourself to always deliver great work. Great work takes a lot of time and preparation. It takes also courage. Courage to develop your own voice. Courage to discover your talent and take it to the maximum of potential.

You have to believe in your work even if you receive no recognition for it. All the successful people I have studied over the years have that common denominator: They work very hard, every single day, fueled by their faith in the cause. They understand the importance of persistence, resilience, and failure. They do not stop at the first obstacles. They see obstacles as opportunities for growth and they untap unexplored paths towards their desired destination.

I also do not believe in good luck. To give all the weight and credit to a single random event and ignore all the years of hard work and determination, is something that simply does not resonate with me. I believe that one is the architect of his or her own destiny; we fabricate our future with the actions we pursue in the present. What we call good luck, is nothing more than the results of hard work manifesting itself into our life.

ACTION:

Think about your talents. What can you do today to become even better at them? How much time can you dedicate every day to work on them? Let's set a challenge: Choose one talent and write down what are you willing to do and how much time you will dedicate every day to make it grow.

Share it with me on Instagram using the hashtag #SuccessWithKnecht

Why preparation is everything

We know that we have latent talents within us and that we have the ability and power to manifest them. However, to remain humble about our capabilities, is the real enabler to keep reaching more superior layers of success. Just look at the nature around us. Nature is the most wonderful and wisest phenomenon we will ever know. It works diligently and precise; subtle and delicate. Nature has no double intentions, or no hurry to show off. It's beauty and wisdom unfold by itself perfectly, precisely, quietly and continuously. The torrent of life has no beginning and no end.

We have still a lot to learn from nature. We tend to minimise its power and wisdom by treating it as a resource for our own means and we forget that it is actually our very source of life.

I see talent as a dormant seed, that is inside of us, waiting to blossom. However, the seed does not transform itself into a tree instantaneously; it requires constant care, continuous and correct feeding; the right soil and light conditions. The seed grows every-day, with no single exception. No seed ever says, 'I have worked enough so I will take some holidays and stop growing for some weeks'. It simply keeps growing at its proper rate. Then suddenly, that small, apparently insignificant dormant seed becomes a majestic tree whose perfect branches and leaves supports and beautifies life for all beings.

People that keep working on themselves, and stay prepared and alert to confront the different situations in life are the people that will succeed. And even if they have reached the top, they keep preparing; they keep learning and keep adapting to the new demands of the world. Remember, the world is a very fast-changing space. Nothing ever remains the same. It is true in nature and it is true for us as well.

Preparation becomes even more important when you have reached your goals. Many successful people have mentioned several times that reaching the top is not the hardest, but maintaining yourself there is the real challenge. A successful person never stops working on their next goals. Like Gary Piper says, "Rest is rust". Preparation means maintaining yourself active. Keep preparing for everything that comes in your way. The best prepared you are, the most likely you will succeed at your endeavours.

A remarkable example of a person who became a self-made genius through intense perseverance in self-improvement and preparation is Benjamin Franklin, one of the founding fathers of the United States. His versatility and level of expertise in diverse areas of human affairs were impressive: From scientist, writer, inventor, politician, activist and industrialist. Franklin firmly believed that he had the moral obligation to become the best version of himself and developed methods to keep himself prepared and disciplined. One of his most famous self-development tools are the Thirteen Virtues. He selected thirteen qualities where he wanted to become better at and dedicated a full week to each of them exclusively. After finishing the last one he would start all over again. He kept working on these virtues over the course of his life. His method has proven to be very successful because it contained the key elements to develop successful habits: focus, observation, tracking and repetition.

We all know that there are certain situations or life events to which you cannot fully prepare. Life often throws us unexpected events. It is simply impossible to prepare for everything. But that doesn't mean that we cannot be prepared at least with our attitude. It is a fact that we cannot control the outside situations, but what we can control is our attitude towards it.

Develop a winning attitude

"Whether you think you can, or think you can't, you are always right."

- Henry Ford

You probably are familiar by now with Donald Trump. Whether you are a fan or not, you might agree with me that he is a person hard to ignore. What thrills me about him is his ability to stir very strong emotions in people, both in a positive and in a negative way. It's a fact of life, whether you are a leader or not, that you will never be a coin of gold for everybody. There will always be people that love you or hate you, but the worst of all, in my opinion, is to be ignored. I think that is by far the worst of feelings we can experience as social creatures. And Donald mastered the art of being everything except ignored.

If you doubt it, just make a small search on internet about how many books about Donald Trump have been written; The New York times estimates that there has been more than four thousand unique book titles about him since he took office; most of those books have been reported to be 'best seller hits'. Michael D'Antonio in his book, *Never Enough: Donald Trump and the Pursuit of Success* even commented that no one in the world of business or modern politics, not Bill Gates, nor Warren Buffet; not even Barak Obama has been as famous as Mr Trump.

As a very controversial character who attracts so much worldwide attention, I felt curious about what a personality like Donald Trump has to say about attitude and what we can learn from him. You might love him or hate him; but we cannot deny that he is an extraordinary phenomenon, that has achieved what most people would never dream of:

not only is he a very successful billionaire businessman, but against all odds, he even became the President of The United States of America between 2016 and 2020. Something almost impossible to achieve if you are an 'outsider' in the very select crew of American politicians.

Donald admits in his autobiography, *The Art of the Deal* that he is a big thinker and he fully believed in the power of displaying a strong winning attitude beyond anything else. He has mentioned on many occasions that the main reason for his success when he was starting his career was purely his strong, positive attitude. From his own words: "Display a big-thinking attitude that shows you are an active, enthusiastic, decisive, efficient, committed, important person who believes in him or herself The simple act of thinking big already distinguishes you from the majority of people".

Another example that demonstrates how having a big and winning attitude can take you far is to take a look at the story of the city of Dubai in the Middle East.

If you happened to visit Dubai in the early seventies, all you would probably have seen is dune after dune in a vast desert, filled with camels and a couple of small fisher villages. The biggest developments you could see at the time were a tiny port called the Dubai Creek, and a small two-way road in the middle of the desert that connected Dubai with Abu Dhabi.

The rulers at the time, Sheik Zayed together with Sheik Rashid, had the vision to convert Dubai into one of the most important cities in the Middle East and a worldwide trading hub; to bring commerce, tourism and inject a vibrant life to this apparently insipid, desertic, hopeless place. They dreamed of creating an equivalent to New York, London, or Shanghai in the Middle East.

In order to make this happen, they thought about starting a project to build the tallest building of the region in the middle of the Dubai desert, develop greenery spaces and big gardens as part of the infrastructure so that more developers would invest there and convert the city from an arid desert into an attractive spot for tourism, living and business.

After years of consultation, several experts rejected the possibility to maintain greenery in the arid desertic conditions of Dubai. They said it was virtually impossible to keep a green ecosystem because of the salty soil conditions typical from the desert, the extreme hot temperatures during summer and the lack of sweet water to keep the gardens alive.

Sheik Zayed and Sheik Rashid, decided not to give up despite the negative outlook from the experts. Sheik Rashid Al Maktoum, current prime minister of Dubai, mentions in his book, *Reflections about Positivity and Happiness* that one of the core personality traits from Sheik Zayed and Sheik Rashid were their unbeatable faith, their visionary and positive outlook of life and their strong, positive attitude when facing challenges and limitations.

They defied all odds by implementing a soil irrigation system that enabled planting of greenery possible, and built a continuous sweet water supply to keep the system working optimally. That was the beginning of a continuous stream of city projects that transformed Dubai from a fisherman small village into one of the most modern and vibrant cities in the world.

I visited Dubai for the first time in 2018 and I was impressed by the stunning infrastructure, the amount of modern skyscrapers, including the tallest building in the world at this time of writing - the Burj Kalifa, the amount of beautiful, well maintained parks and greenery; and the high level, sophisticated urban transport and other facilities that the city offers. No wonder why Dubai is nowadays one of the most visited cities in the Middle East and probably of the world which attracts more than fifteen million tourists a year.

How can such an insignificant, small town in the middle of the desert transform into the most important city in the Middle East and one of the most important trading hubs of the world in just a couple of decades? They even have a snow skiing facility for God's sake!

It definitely took something else besides the rich amount of oil reserves and the natural resources extracted from the sea. Someone had a vision for the city that went beyond the common imagination; and then injected a strong leadership fueled with positive attitude to make it happen.

From the words of Sheik Rashid Al Maktoum: "Our existence is not the consequence of a casualty, nor we adapted to the circumstances of our environment. We created our own circumstances and our own success. I am not saying this to show off, or as a response to the media, but to inspire future generations to continue this path with the same spirit, the same determination, and the same persistence. The closest we have been to have good luck has been the fighting spirit and the passion to overcome the challenges that passes through our veins positive people know that the good luck does not happen to them but that they themselves create their own good luck".

Going after your biggest dreams will be the scariest thing you will pursue in this life. No one can nor will guarantee you success. The world owes you nothing. If you want to make it big, you have to demonstrate to the world the value you can bring. You have to believe in yourself before anyone else will. You have to develop an enduring faith in you, in your God-given capabilities, and believe that the vision you are pursuing is worthwhile living for and fighting for.

No one knows what you are all capable of. And most people, frankly, do not care. You are the only person who knows and who cares. The best way to present yourself toward others is displaying a great attitude. If you believe you can do it, others will believe it too!

Be the best and learn from the best

If you are already doing something, why not to aspire to do your best?

In this world, we need and praise hierarchies of competence. There is no doubt that all men are made equal and possess the same intrinsic human rights. But when it comes to human activity, there are certain levels of competence in every sector of human affairs. We have a vast number of professions that we aspire to do. We have doctors, lawyers, teachers, plumbers, artists, writers, dancers, cookers and so on. Within those professions, we have those that we consider the best; the eminent doctors, talented architects, creative writers and we also have mediocre ones.

Think about it. In which level do you place yourself? Do you want to do something just to pass the time and go home, or do you want to do something meaningful for this world and for others?

When we aspire to be the best, we will push ourselves to the limit. We will find meaning in our profession. We will discover many other ways to be great at what we do. To aspire just to get a degree, or to get a job just for the sake of earning money and afford things, without the aspiration to become the best, it would be merely a mediocre acceptance of life. It will not fulfil you. You will need additional 'sources of pleasure' like alcohol, food, sex, entertainment to fill out the emptiness of a frustrated profession.

That's why I find it fundamental to pay attention to your heart and find out what you really love doing. Only when you do what you love, you will have automatically the burning desire to do always your very best; you will develop the work ethic of working hard, getting disciplined, learning how to overcome the struggles of the job, and convert some plain profession into something beautiful. You will no longer need to fool yourself with productivity curses, life hack tips to avoid procrastination and anything of the sort. *Only love knows how to work at the highest levels of excellence.*

Society praises hierarchies of competence. When you have a terminal illness, you don't want just a mediocre doctor to treat your illness. You want the best doctor to look after you. When you go on a special holiday and want to eat something you don't want to go to a simple restaurant. You want to go to the best restaurant in town. You want your local football team to be the best team. You want to get the best that life can offer. If it would be just okay to get mediocre things, what could we possibly aspire for? What is the reason for doing anything at all?

Not only is important to aspire for the best, but it also helps to look after people that are already the best in their fields and learn from them. You want to be a great film producer? Learn from the best. You want to be a great hip hop dancer? Find the best in town and ask for mentorship. You want to be a great mother? Look after someone you admire and observe what she does and how she does it.

You don't have to start from zero to reach a desired goal. Go, investigate and get in contact with people that already did what you want to do. Learn from them. Work for them. Observe closely what are the personal attributes this person has, that you need to develop in yourself. Look at every single detail of his/ her actions, words, physical manners, etc. The idea is not to copy exactly the person, but to get inspiration about how to develop your own capabilities by following the best possible examples.

172

You are already following and being influenced by people either consciously or unconsciously. So, why not to do a conscious effort to follow the very best?

"If you want the best the world has to offer, offer the world your best."

- Neale Donald

#TheKnechtWay to exploit your talents

Everybody is born with unique talents. Your job is to discover yours and let them blossom at the highest of levels:

- Decide for yourself how serious you want to work on your talents. Do you want to be a meteor, a planet, or a fixed star like the sun?
- Remember that talent is just 1% and preparation is 99% of the success formula.
- Preparation is everything. Even after discovering your talents and reaching the top, you must always prepare yourself for what might and will come.
- Display a strong positive attitude. This will help you in keeping your energies focused in finding new ways to do things and getting better results.
- Good luck does not come from the sky. Good luck comes from hard work, determination, perseverance and a strong, positive and competent attitude.
- Society praises levels of hierarchy. Aspire to be the best in your profession.
- If you want to be the best in what you do, learn from the best!

BONUS: Interested to know more about how to develop further your talents and improve your ability to do so? Check out the bonus checklist with 10 strategies to boost your abilities; available in the downloadable booklet from The Success Mindset webpage.

Questions for Reflection

1. *Do you know what your talents are?*

2. *What can you do to use your talents in the most productive and positive way?*

3. *What other personality traits can help you to develop your talents and reach success?*

4. *What are you willing to give up from your life right now so you can achieve your biggest goals?*

5. *How can you bring your profession to the next level and become the best in class?*

"Only love knows how to work at the highest levels of excellence."

Paola Knecht

Ninth Pillar

Develop a Strong Resilience

*B*uilding a strong resilience is the ninth pillar for developing the success mindset.

When I think about resilience, the person that comes to my mind that truly represents this word is Nelson Mandela.

His personal biography is one of the most touching and incredible ones I have ever read. I have heard about resilience before. It was a concept I understood and I thought it was a good quality to have as a leader, and in general, resilience has become a trending trait because it has to do with the ability to cope with change and difficult situations. In other words, resilience means to keep going, to remain calm in the middle of the storm.

However, only when I have read the story of Nelson is when the word 'resilience' really took a deeper meaning inside of me. Nelson Mandela, born in 1918 in the region of Transkei, was a cheerful boy, who grew up having a 'normal life' in his little town in Mvezo. His interest in politics emerged as a teenager, when working for the CNA (National African Congress) doing first simple jobs like messenger or as an assistant during the congregations.

With the time, he realised that the reality of his country as a black person, did not had really a promising future. As he describes in his memoir, he did not had any special calling or a hunch that told him he should leave everything and fight for his country; but the everyday mistreatments and attacks toward his people is what made him accumulate the enough courage and determination to rebel and dedicate his energies to the liberation of his country.

He literally spent all his life in this fight. The way to freedom was not the easiest one. He confronted several obstacles along the way, including living many years under hiding, when trying to form an army to fight against the oppressive actions of the police, led by the government. His family was threatened several times. His office and house set on fire. He spent twenty-seven years in prison in the most inhumane conditions. When reading his story, (which I recommend to anyone interested in great leadership and what it takes to be an extraordinary human being), I came to think several times: How can a human being deal with so much pain, so much humiliation, so much oppression, continuously and permanently for so long to fight against a dream, an ideal with no guarantee at all of success?

That is for me, the biggest lesson on resilience.

During his time in prison, even knowing that the risk of getting a perpetual condemnation and the possibility to die in prison was high, he still maintained a fighting spirit.

"I was behind the bars, but I also knew that I was not willing to abandon the cause. This will continue here, in different circumstances and in a more restricted manner. A terrain where the only public will be us and our oppressors. We considered the fight on the prison like a micro-cosmos of the overall fight. We will combat it on the inside, as we would on the outside."

- Nelson Mandela

The rest is history. He became the first black president in South Africa. He won the Nobel Prize for Peace together with F.W. de Klerk for successfully collaborating in the eradication of the Apartheid Era in that country. He ended up being one of the most loved and respected leaders in the world. To this very day, I doubt there has been other like him. With his charisma, humility, cleverness and infinite perseverance to fight for his dream, he became a legend and the icon of resilience of our era.

Another extraordinary example of resilience is the story of Edith Eger, a ninety-three-year-old psychologist and a holocaust survivor. She understood very early in life the meaning of keeping a strong positive attitude, despite the hardships that life threw at her. To say that she experienced hardships is already a very mild statement, taking into account what she has been through since a very young age.

In 1944 at the age of sixteen, she lost her parents and everything she had, when the Gestapo broke into her home in Hungary and took them to the concentration camps in Auschwitz. The horrors she experienced in the concentration camps are beyond any human comprehension in the modern days: extreme hunger, sickness, extreme colds, the sensation that every moment could be the last moment of your life; the terror of seeing death so close, so present; so pervasive cleaning human teeth, hair and skin from the gas chambers became an everyday task. The terrible scenery is enough justification to let yourself surrender to the circumstances, to wait for your death and nothing else. But Edith thought differently. She fought for her life by taking the decision to picture a different scenario in her mind. She and her sister Klara constructed a parallel mental world that allowed them to remain curious, resilient, patient and strong even some sparks of cheerfulness they could show by creating mental stories, victories, imaginary dinners and reunions within themselves.

Her autobiographical book *La Bailarina de Auschwitz* or the English original *The choice: Embrace the possible* is a wonderful gift for the soul. It gives you the opportunity to learn from first-hand experience of an holocaust survivor, to confront one of the most prominent but suppressed human experiences: Suffering. How to deal with big loses? How to learn to forgive? Not only to those who hurt us, but also learn how to forgive ourselves.

Edith and her sister Klara survived the concentration camps because they maintained at all times a strong willingness to live: "Do not ruin your spirit, enlighten it like a torch!" She kept saying this whenever she was confronted with life and death situations. After her liberation, she moved to the United States and eventually obtained the doctorate in Psychology. Edith has been contributing ever since to helping people get through their traumas with the practice of logotherapy. One of her most remarkable life lessons she shares in her book is that our life experiences are not a handicap, like we often think, but they are a gift. They provide us with perspective and meaning, and gives us unique opportunities to redefine our life objectives and our strength to make it happen.

You too, can develop a strong resilience

The stories of Nelson Mandela and Edith Eger are as inspiring as they are intimidating. However, you do not need to spend twenty-seven years in prison or go through the extreme circumstances of the holocaust to develop a strong level or resilience.

Recent scientific studies have shown that resilience gets supported by a neuroplastic process that occurs in our brains; which means, that it can be learned over time. However, from a metaphysical perspective, we also know that a child is born with 'knowledge', an inborn attitude towards persons and some elements of the environment via genetic inheritance. As living entities, we have within ourselves already the inborn trait of *succeeding*; making reference again to a baby, which is by definition a human in development, which is not yet fully conscious of the proper sense of his Self, still shows within himself the capability of acquiring information, learning, decoding and acting based on his exposures to the environment; all with the objective of survival. So, from our birth, we already have within ourselves the seed of resilience, which has been a key element for our survival as species.

If resilience is something that is partly learned and partly inherited, why some people is more resilient than others?

When we were kids, most of our educational structure has been based on punishments & rewards. If we were good kids, and we did everything our parents or teachers told us, we get a reward. If we were rebels and acted against what was expected from us, we got punished. We learned over the years to be docile to authority and to trust other's opinions more than our own.

It is not surprising to see that we start to lose over the years the connection to our inner-strengths; to that inborn resilience. If someone tells you that you have failed, you believe it more than you challenge it. Even if that person does not know you and have no idea about your journey. We stumble towards the so-called critics and experts and if we don't perform according to their expectations, we feel vanished.

If we keep performing according to other's expectations, and we constantly approve it and believe it as truth, our brain reinforces those thought patterns so strongly that over time, it starts to be pretty normal to act at the expense of others.

To stop this, we need to observe and detect those behaviours. Am I acting out of an automatic earned response, or am I really listening to my gut and putting my own thinking first?

In order to connect back to your inborn resilience and develop it further to adapt it to the new circumstances of the environment, you would need to be exposed to the possibility to face fear and ridicule, and still have the courage to keep moving forward. Instead of giving up and moving to something else, if you keep insisting, and trying, your mind will get trained again to embrace those challenging situations.

David Goggins, ex-Navy Seal and Guinness Record winner athlete, summarises pretty well this last idea: "It's important to push hardest when you want to quit the most is because it helps you to callous your mind".

How to develop more resilience

When you think about the meaning of resilience: "the capacity to re-cover quickly from difficulties; and the ability to mentally and emo-tionally cope with a crisis", you might be asking: How can I do this? How can I build my resilience? How can I become stronger and remain calm while dealing with the many adversities life will throw at me?

As we briefly discussed in our sixth pillar, resilience can be re-learned. It is a matter of decision, courage and discipline.

The best way to develop more resilience is to fully participate on the arena. In other words, go out there and get your work exposed. Get out and talk your mind; go after what you want.

You will experience disappointments, you will be exposed to failure and maybe even to ridicule. That is what you need, to get your mind trained again in how to overcome disappointments.

"Whenever I get faced with a difficult decision, I ask myself: What would I do if I weren't afraid of making a mistake, feeling rejected, looking foolish or being alone?"

- Oprah Winfrey

The thing we fear the most when we are dealing with a difficult situation or a crisis, is the pain. As human beings, we have learned that we should stay away from the pain and try to look out only for pleasant experiences. That's why when we are confronted with a potential or real risky situation, our body triggers a response in form of physical or emotional pain. However, not all the pain we experience is the same.

There are two main forms we can experience pain. The first form of pain is *a priori*, which is the pain we suffer when we think about a potential danger before being exposed to it yet.

And then we have the pain *a posteriori*, which is the one you suffer as a result of doing a particular action; it can be that you failed at something, you lost something or you experience a physical pain after a hard physical training.

The pain *a priori* is completely useless and it often ends up in stopping us doing the activity related to the triggering of the pain. It is for example, the pain you experience the moment before doing a big speech in public, or before doing that difficult call to a boss or a client. The fear of experiencing the pain becomes the dominant emotion and you end up not doing the activity at all, postponing it or finding an excuse why not to do it.

The pain *a posteriori* is on the other hand, completely necessary and it is the one where we should focus our effort in learning to manage it. If we get to manage the pain that results from action, we are building our muscle of resilience. Let's take the example of physical pain experienced as a result of a rigorous training. When I set my running goal, I try as much as possible to increase the amount of kilometres and reduce the amount of time that I spend running in order to increase my performance.

Let's say that I decided to run two kilometres extra from the normal routine. While I am running at the usual trail, my body recognises and experiences the sensations of the known path. At a certain point in time when I have reached the usual known path, my body starts to alert me that is time to stop; I start to get faster breathing, my legs start to hurt. By my pure sheer of will, I overwrite the command of my brain and tell my body to keep running.

My body starts complaining and I start to experience physical pain; my brain starts to play ugly games and starts to tell me that I should stop, that I am tired, that my legs are hurting, my breath is getting more difficult despite the pain, I kept running. Then there is a point in time when my mind and body together enter into a trance state. I feel the pain, but I don't interiorise it, I just observe it. I keep my mind focused on the end mark. I keep saying I can do it. When I reach my desired goal, I rest, I feel the sensation of my body, I feel the relieved pain after the extra work but suddenly is not hurting anymore.

If I set the routine to keep running those extra two kilometres every running session, I struggle in the first few runs until my mind connects the new trail as the 'usual path'. Suddenly, after a couple of sessions, I end up running those extra two kilometres with no problems at all. Which means, my body had built resilience on the extra challenge and now sees it as a normal behaviour.

I have experienced the same sort of resilience whenever I do a painful task. For example, I hated to speak on the phone. It caused me some sort of nervousness or fear, to speak to someone I cannot see on the other side of the line. As a way to overcome this pain, I decided to get into the habit of calling someone I don't know three times a day; it might be for doing an appointment, or randomly ask a question whatever it came to my mind, but I had to always make the calls. The first few days I felt like I was in a living nightmare and the pure thought of waking up and knowing I had to make three calls nauseated me. But after four or five days, the feeling started disappearing. My mind embraced the new activity as a 'known path'. I believe the same happens when you are often exposed in doing all other kind of activities. After you do it enough times, your body and mind adapt them as the 'new normal'.

Resilience is a wonderful inborn mechanism that you can use in your favour to accomplish what you aspire in life. If you use it wisely, it can take you very far!

ACTION:

Let's train your resilience muscle. Think of a situation that you dislike and feel uncomfortable with. Now challenge yourself to confront this situation at least once a day for five days. For example, if you try to avoid chit chatting with people you don't know, make the effort to do it once a day for the next five days. How did it go?

Don't forget to share your thoughts with me on Instagram with the hashtag #SuccessWithKnecht

Dealing with Pressure

If you have been looking for a job recently, you might have read in the job adds the following cliché sentence: *The individual that aims for the job must have the ability to work under a lot of pressure*. Reading that sentence alone made you feel already under pressure, isn't it?

When you say, 'I feel under pressure', what is exactly what you feel? Pressure from what? Pressure from whom? Pressure, if we think about it, is nothing more than an anxious feeling of needing to cope with a bunch of external expectations, either created by you or by the environment surrounding you. When looking at the pure physical, scientific definition of pressure, we find out that pressure is "a force applied perpendicular to the surface of an object per unit area over which that force is distributed". If you translate that technical- looking meaning in a psychological metaphor, the forces you feel while being under pressure are the commands, desires, needs and requests from people related to you in a way, which are expecting something from you.

Nowadays, dealing with pressure is no longer a luxury for the high paying jobs and leadership positions, although the request for dealing with pressure in such jobs is much higher. We know that dealing with pressure is an inevitable part of living in a collective society where you have to deal with many individuals with different needs and desires, and being part of a collective society makes you immediately a target of being a medium by which others can reach their goals.

However, we know that pressure in the mindset of a person is merely a 'feeling' rather than a physical act. That means, that you have the freedom, the power and the capability to deal with the feeling in any way you want. Most people don't think that they *have a choice,* but they do!

186

You may not be able to prevent that people approach you to get something from you. Depending on the nature of your job and the kind of life you have, you might be exposed to more demands or less. If you have a job where the outcome you produce has an impact on hundreds or even thousands of people, the perceived level of pressure is higher than if the impact of your actions only affects a couple of people. Whether big or small, the feeling by itself is sometimes unavoidable, but you can choose how to deal with it.

If you are really serious about being successful, you have to be able to handle pressure well. Life is a series of unexpected events, and nobody will ever have the certainty about what will happen in the future. It can be that in some periods of time you are striving and having a wonderful time, but other times you will be touching the ground and nothing goes your way.

The art of dealing with pressure comes from the act of performing towards your desired direction, maintaining a positive mental state and acting with conviction and faith navigating through the storms other people create, and still manage to keep the boat (mental peace) under control.

Nelson Mandela never lost his boat. He went through all kinds of hardships and was even condemned for twenty-seven years of prison due to his unwavering convictions. He overcame the fear of going to prison, the fear of ridicule, even the fear of death, and developed an extraordinary resilient mentality, which kept him going. He managed to keep calm and focused and did not get overwhelmed with pressure in an era where the faith of an entire nation was perceived to lay on his shoulders.

His resilience backed him up with a strong faith and love for his cause, and kept his boat going. The enormous undertaking definitely paid off. Edith Eger could survive one of the most horrible events in human history when she was still a teenager because she decided not to invest her precious mind in death and fatality, but rather on life, faith and love.

We all have the capability of being resilient. See yourself as a precious diamond that is hidden in a bunch of dark carbon. All you have to do is to put yourself on the right pressure, the right conditions and then work diligently in getting polished, and you will transform yourself in a beautiful and brilliant gemstone.

Turn pressure as your ally instead of your enemy. Let the pressure be the fuel that sets you in action mode. Remember, dealing with the right amount of pressure can turn you into a diamond!

#TheKnechtWay to build resilience

Resilience is the capacity to maintain a positive mental and physical state during stressful and difficult situations; it's also the capacity to recover quickly from setbacks:

- Resilience is an inborn trait; however due to our educational system we learn to suppress it. To build the muscle of resilience back, you need to get comfortable dealing with the pain that results from action; for example, the pain experienced after a rejection, a loss or a physical pain.

- There are other instances in which pain is not helpful; for example, the psychological pain experienced before taking action. This type of pain should be eliminated, otherwise it freezes action.

- Resilience used in a good way helps the neuronal system to develop new connections; is what in other terms we call new learnings, new abilities and skills;

- A healthy amount of pressure is necessary to keep focus and calibrate our energies towards the desired goals.

- Big responsibilities require to take bigger amounts of pressure. The best way to learn and test what is your limit, is by taking bigger and bigger responsibilities, one at a time.

Exercises for Reflection

1. *Recall a situation where you experienced a big amount of physical or mental pain. What was the reason behind the pain? How could you have used the pain as a way to build up more resilience?*

2. *Think of a decision that you need to make but haven't been able to. What is stopping you? What kind of pain could be related to your choice of no making the decision? How can you change it?*

3. *Think about your life in general. Do you feel challenged all the time? Are you getting a lot of requests from other people? How can you channel the pressure in a way to builds up your resilience storage?*

4. *What can you do today that can help you build mental resilience?*

Tenth Pillar

To be grateful is to be present

*D*o you know what it feels to surrender yourself to this very moment?

You probably think this is an odd question, but give it a thought: Have you ever experienced being in the here and now without any perception of time, and any perception of identity? Just feeling your body, the senses and emotions that the current moment are triggering in you most of us ignore those small details of the present. More often than not we are trapped in a sleepy state, wandering our thoughts between the past and the future, with no regards to the present.

We also think that by staying focused on the future is the way to become prosperous. Here makes sense to remind us again that everything that comes to pass in the future, is the result of what we are doing at this precise moment. When you experience gratitude in what is happening now in all dimensions of your life, you are bringing the real prosperity. Life is a series of moments and every moment brings by itself the seed of potentiality of all you can become. Our thoughts dominate our lives.

When our thoughts are too focused on events that have happened or that are about to happen, we completely miss what is really going on in our lives. To be fully in the present, means to pay attention to what is happening around you right now: where are you standing? What do you see in your surroundings? What are the smells you perceive in the place where you are right now? What are the sensations of your body?

As James Allen said in his book, *As a Man Thinketh:* "Men imagine that their thoughts can be kept secret, but it cannot; it rapidly crystalises into habit and habit solidifies its circumstances". What you see around you, is the reflection of your thoughts.

Gratitude is one of the most powerful tools we have to focus on the present. There is a popular saying that we do not attract what we want, but we attract what we are. A grateful heart will attract more of what you feel grateful for: more health, more wealth, more creativity more plenitude.

Get into the habit of being grateful for everything that happens in your life; Be thankful for the good moments that make you feel happy and complete; and for the bad moments that are wise teachers and show you the direction for opportunities of change. Both the good and the bad moments are motives for feeling genuinely grateful.

Show gratitude every day

Oprah Winfrey, in her book, *What I Know For Sure* said that she kept a gratitude diary for over a decade, and encourages everybody to do the same: "I know for sure that appreciating whatever shows up for you in life changes your whole world. You radiate and generate more goodness for yourself when you're aware of all you have and not focusing on your have-nots."

There are many small ways how you can express gratitude daily. It can be something so simple as keeping a gratitude journal like Oprah, or saying thank you to every person that did a favour to you during the day. What really matters is to be sincere in your gratitude towards life and the Creator. To be sincerely and authentically grateful for everything that honours your life, big and small, is what will really have a lasting impact in your life.

I have personally kept a journal for over twenty years. In this journal, I have written not only about all my experiences, but also, I had the habit to write down all the things I was grateful for, even if the experience itself was not a positive one. When something at school, work or with my relationships did not happen as I expected, I thanked for the situation because they always taught me something valuable about myself and about life. When I look back to what I have written twenty years ago about who I was, what I had, and compare it with today, I see with astonishment how wonderfully everything has unfolded. I definitely got much more than I dreamed of at the time, and I feel amazed how grateful I was back then with so little.

I personally love the idea of keeping a gratitude journal for the wonderful effects it has brought to my life. But there are many other ways you can practice your gratitude daily. For example:

- Doing something small for someone

- Give a compliment to someone you don't know

- Feel happy about the food at your table

- Smile to everyone who passes by

- Go for a walk in nature and breathe deep the fresh air; walk into the fresh soil with your bare feet

- Pray with gratitude before going to bed and/or before starting the day

- Sit in silence for a couple of minutes and feel the breeze, let yourself feel in complete calm and smile sincerely to yourself

To experience gratitude is to live in a state of grace; is to recognise the miracle of life and to be sincerely thankful for being part of it. Gratitude is also confirmation of faith; a surrendering state to what really exist now, which is all it can be and will ever be.

If you like the idea of keeping a gratitude journal, you can download a free gratitude journal template in the booklet available on the book's website.

The present moment is all we have

Eckhart Tolle is right when he says that the only thing we have is the now. We might be wandering in our minds between past and future elaborations of reality, but essentially you are still here. Your body is here and not in your past or future. You are breathing at this very moment. You are reading these words right now. Everything you are, have been and will ever be is happening right now. Tomorrow does not exist. The past is gone. The future is constantly in the making, and those actions are happening now. Many authors, psychologist, spiritualists and scientist have been obsessed with the studies of time and space for centuries and the only conclusion they all agree on, is that time-space is a human construction that only exist now.

You don't need to do any elaborate studies, complicated experiments, sophisticated planning or any other extraordinary activity to realise this simple truth: What you are doing right now, will determine what you will be doing tomorrow and how your future will unfold. The present is the continuous life state; the moment of now contains in itself eternity because eternity can only exist now. What you do now is what you will be tomorrow.

In our current society we put way too much faith on 'predictions' and 'forecasts with numbers' from other people when we are trying to figure out the future. We believe all sorts of experts, gurus, future tellers and spiritual celebrities of the like. We love to read horoscopes, watch predictions on the news, read messages in Chinese fortune teller cookies and even go as far as paying enormous amounts of money for any product and service that promises us future health, eternal beauty, long lasting happiness if you don't believe me, just look at how vastly rich the insurance, entertainment and health industries are.

We could save ourselves a lot of time and money if we would just focus on the right now and recognise who we really are. What are you doing right now? How are you feeling right now? What do you need to change right now? Answer for yourself those questions, take action, and I guarantee you, you will be heading in the right direction. No fortune-teller cookie needed!

I can almost hear from afar your next question. Okay, Paola, that all sounds nice. But how do I actually manage to *stay* in the present?

For most of us, our mind is like a little wild child, spreading its thoughts here and there, apparently with little or no control whatsoever. Like most things in life, being present is something we inherently have in our human nature but has been completely forgotten in the name of progress and education.

Being present is something we need to re-learn and consciously apply. Some practices that are very good starting points with reconnecting to your present are:

- Meditation: Reserve some minutes of your day to sit quietly and let your mind wander away. With enough practice and dedication, you will start to identify those moments of stillness within you.

194

- Mindfulness: Executing an activity with your full focus and attention brings you back to the present moment. Make an effort to put a lot of focus on your small routinary activities and see how you feel. For example, pay the closest attention to something as simple as when eating an apple. What are the sensations you experience when you bite it? How does it taste? How do you feel while eating it? Feel the intensity of the moment. You might discover that there is so much profundity in small things than you could ever have imagined! Remember that curiosity and observation are the seeds of genius.

- Silence: Especially on a busy day, schedule a few minutes where you can sit and stay by yourself. Just look at the surroundings. What do you see? How does the air smell? What is running through your mind? Sit and observe.

- Connect to nature: Nothing can bring you closer to the present than to admire a beautiful sunset, feel the breeze of the air in the forest, hug a tree and feel his vital energy, admire a beautiful flower, gaze at the fantastic mountains, hear the birds sing nature gives us thousands of opportunities every day to connect. To connect with nature is to be in the present.

The compound effect

Doing small actions every day have a compound effect. This term is widely used in the financial sector to describe what happens to every dollar you invest at a certain interest rate which keeps being reinvested and accumulating earnings over every dollar invested over time. We can apply the same concept to the small actions we are investing every day in the fulfilment of our goals. Darren Hardy, author of the book, The *Compound Effect* defines it as a strategy to reap big rewards from small, seemingly insignificant actions performed consistently over a period of time.

Taking advantage of the compound effect, we could plan our day in a way that every activity that we perform goes in relation to fulfiling our goals and the kind of life we want for ourselves. Like we discussed in previous sections of the book, success is not a result of one single action, or a lucky event that happens randomly. Success is the result of a consistent set of actions performed over time in a way that keeps you moving forward.

Think about the endless hours of training that elite athletes invest every day for years, to prepare for a single event, like the Olympic games or a World championship. Think about the mother who invest restless nights over several months in order to keep breastfeeding their babies as long as possible so they can grow healthy and strong. Every great effort and achievement come from the seeds of small actions, consistency, perseverance and an unwavering focus on what is being done in the present.

Observing nature can show us yet again how perfectly the compound effect works. An Oak tree takes around thirty to forty years to grow. At the time of planting the seed, several weeks and months can pass by without noticing any apparent movement on the soil. Suddenly, a small stem will eventually show out off the ground 'out of the blue'. This small stem over time will convert itself into a full grown mature tree that can reach up to three meters high and can produce fruit and acorn for the next forty years. Oak trees can live as long as three hundred years! Who would have thought, that such a tiny seed planted in the soil, will convert itself from a tiny oval into a majestic Oak tree that last centuries?

Nature is a majestic teacher full of wisdom. Observe the works of nature and you will get very valuable insights about how life works. If you have a goal, a dream, a vision but feel lost and do not know how to start, do it like nature: Start small. Start doing small and humble actions that bring order into your life to give you a sense of accomplishment. Get up early, do your bed, maintain order in your living space. Write down your dreams, fantasise and write down how to get there. Then decide what will you do today to reach them. It can be a small thing like writing an email, get subscribed on to a course, call a friend, go out and do some sport; read some books and invest in getting yourself as much educated as possible. Do all those small things repeatedly and consistently and after fifteen years you will be unbeatable!

"The grandeur of life cannot be reached by doing one big punctual effort, but it can be reached by doing many small punctual efforts."

- Raimon Samsó

Your actions today have a big impact in your life and the life of others

In western cultures, we like to see ourselves as *individuals:* a logo, a person being one entity, out of the seven billion that inhabit our world today; excluding our fellow neighbours from other species. We don't see any apparent connection to others except for the obvious ones, which are our closest family relatives and friends. The feelings of loneliness and hopelessness come from this belief, that you are 'standing alone against the world'. Looking at human nature and human reality from this perspective, creates the perception of division: We are just one single point in the universe, standing for ourselves. "I belong to a small group and beyond that group nothing concerns me". When you believe you are just one small point in the whole world, then you probably think that what you do or say do not have much importance in the overall sense of things, as you are just a small speck in this vast planet.

But what if we change this perspective, and see ourselves as a network instead? You are one link on the vast network. Let's say that you know and interact with at least thousand people during your life as up to now. Those thousand people with which you interact, know other thousand people themselves and those know other thousand and so goes on. That means, you are one person away from one million people and two persons away from one billion!

Do you see how important you are in this vast network? What you do and say, will resonate millions of people away in a direct or indirect way. That's why our small actions and even our smallest of thoughts have a heavy weight in the great scheme of things. Knowing this powerful truth, you should make it as your duty to be very meaningful about what you say and do. As we have been reviewing throughout the book, you have the ability to change your reality and the reality of others with the simplest of your actions. A smile you give on the bus to someone may brighten the day to this person, and as a consequence this person will smile to others and will spread kindness to others and this will multiply a thousand times. You have the choice to speak your mind and thoughts, and pay the price it comes with it as so it will resonate in the network.

Do not underestimate the power of now. Every time you catch yourself on boredom or hopelessness during your day, remember this: Right now, you are an influence for thousands of people. How do you choose to handle this responsibility? Spreading love and hope, or shame and fear?

"Peace can be made only by those who are peaceful, and love can be shown only by those who love. No work of love will flourish out of guilt, fear or hollowness of heart, just as no valid plans for the future can be made by those who have not capacity for living now."

- Alan Watts

#TheKnechtWay to stay present and be grateful

Every great achievement starts in the present:

- What you are thinking today determines how your future will be tomorrow.

- Not paying attention of what you are doing in the present will take away the opportunity to build your future the way you want it.

- What you see today as your life, is the result of what were your thoughts in the past.

- Gratitude is a powerful act to stay in the present.

- The more you feel grateful about life, the more life will give you more of what you feel grateful for.

- Improve your level of presence in the now by doing meditation, walks in nature, and practicing mindfulness.

- Greatness is not achieved by doing one big action, but is the accumulation of small actions done over a long period of time.

- Even your smallest of actions, have a great effect in the vast network of humanity. Take the responsibility of sharing meaningful words and actions that can shape the lives of others in the most subtle of ways.

Exercises for Reflection

1. *Describe a situation when you felt fully and completely in the present. Where were you? What did you see? How did it smell? Try to recall it as vivid as possible.*

2. *Being present requires just one thing: Choose to do it now. Stop what you are doing now and spend the next two minutes just sitting and observing. How did it go? What were your thoughts? What did you feel?*

3. *Reflect and list three other things you could do to practice being in the present.*

4. *How can you connect what you are doing right now with your North Star?*

5. *What changes you need to do in your life so you can experience it more intensely, in the now?*

"The present is the continuous life state; the moment of now contains in itself eternity because eternity can only exist now. What you do now is what you will be tomorrow."

Paola Knecht

Eleventh Pillar

Taking care of body, mind and spirit

*T*he last pillar I want to share with you, is about taking care of your machinery, its whole equipment and the Self that 'inhabits' in it: your body, mind, and spirit.

Let's start with the body. If you want to be successful and achieve great things in life, you definitely need a lot of vitality and energy. You need to be in good physical and mental shape in order to deal with the big hurdles that will come on your way on your journey to reach your Vision.

I am not an expert in nutrition, but I want to share with you what I have learned through my experiences.

Our body is our temple. We only get one single body for our entire journey in this world. It is in our responsibility to maintain it at top condition at all times. That's why the popular saying, *'tell me what you eat and I will tell you who you are'* is not so far from the truth.

The body, our fascinating home, is a living organism with biochemical and bioelectrical functions which interact with everything in the environment. We are not separate entities from it. We are part of it. Therefore, everything that is around us has a direct effect on our health and in our wellbeing.

You are what you eat

A healthy diet is what keeps our body functioning in optimal condition. That's why it's very important to nourish it with the highest-quality food that is possible. Most nutritionists agree that the healthiest type of diet is the one that is mainly whole food plant-based, which include a wide variety of fresh, whole, unprocessed foods like fruits, raw vegetables, nuts and grains. Ideally, it should be free of toxic chemicals and should be organic (not genetically modified). Most nutritionists recommend that foods should be minimally processed (that includes cooking), because all forms of processing reduce their nutritional content. So, try to eat as much raw fresh fruit and veggies as possible!

Drinking water is as well a key element to maintain good health. Keeping the body hydrated is very important so that your body can keep producing the right level of antioxidants, which keeps it healthy and free of radicals. Doctors recommend often eight to nine glasses of water a day. I'm on the idea that you should also listen to your own body and drink water when you feel thirst. As Lester and Parker emphasise in their book, *What really makes you ill? Why Everything You Thought You Knew About Disease is Wrong*: "Dehydration causes the body to become 'stressed', which increases the generation of free radicals that can induce oxidative stress and lead to free radical damage, the underlying mechanism common to virtually all conditions of ill-health, especially chronic conditions".

Mineral compounds are as well crucial to maintain our pH balance in optimal condition. Therefore, you should consume a diet that includes the right level of magnesium, calcium and potassium. Alkaline foods help to reduce the levels of acid in our body, keeping it on the right balance.

Why is it important to keep a diet that is more alkaline than acid? According to a recent study from the Journal of Environmental and Public Health titled *The Alkaline Diet, is there an evidence that Alkaline pH diet benefits health?* present the conclusion that when the body has an imbalance, the acid decreases the supply of oxygen available to all your body's cells and tissues. The lack of oxygen affects the mitochondrial function of the cells, which means that their ability to repair and replenish by themselves becomes impaired; the cells do not receive enough oxygen and nutrients. The result is that your body ages more quickly and as well you feel more fatigue.

Nutritionists recommend a diet that is eighty percent alkaline and twenty percent acidic. Chopra and Snyder in their book, *Radical Beauty* provide a very comprehensive list of alkaline and acidic types of food that you should consume in the recommended quantity.

They recommend to consume eighty percent of the following foods which have varying grades of alkalinity:

- Green vegetables

- Root vegetables (acorn, butternut or coquina squash, yams, turnips, sweet potatoes, etc.)

- All other veggies

- Fruit

- Gluten-free grains (quinoa, brown rice, and steel-cut oats from a gluten-free facility soaked overnight)

- Herbs (parsley, coriander, basil, etc.

- Sprouts

- Seeds (especially chia)

- Nuts, especially almonds and walnuts

- Ginger, turmeric, and other roots that can act as spices in food

- Legumes, such as lentils (in moderation)

- Spices (paprika, cumin, etc.)

You can basically eat plenty from all of the above foods, with the security that your body will receive enough nutrients and will keep its balance right.

Twenty percent of your diet can include acidic foods which you should consume in moderation, or as less as possible. Those are:

- Red meat
- Poultry
- Fish
- Dairy (in all forms, including yoghurt)
- Eggs
- Coffee
- Alcohol (minimise as much as possible)
- Processed foods

I'm not a doctor nor a health expert, but I can share with you my experiences and learnings of following the recommended balance intake between alkaline and acidic foods. Among some of the benefits that are expected are:

- Better oxygen circulation in the body

- Increase of nutrient absorption

- Radiant skin

- Transition from limp to thick hair

- Boundless energy

A little word of caution: before following any specific diet, consult with your doctor or your nutritionist on what is the best approach for you!

Healthy movement

The benefits of regular exercise have been exposed and discussed in all the medical, nutritional and sport fields, so I will be short here. I believe that keeping your body in movement is life.

Mahatma Gandhi, in his autobiography, *The Story of My Experiments with The Truth* came to that conclusion from his own personal experience: "It was mainly this habit of long walks that kept me practically free from illness throughout my stay in England and gave me a fairly strong body".

I personally like to take a walk or go jogging every day in the forest or in a nearby park. To me it feels like a therapy where I can recharge my energy. Of course, any kind of physical activity can only bring benefits to your overall wellbeing.

I am not a health expert as mentioned, but based on my own research and experience, I can share with you some of the great benefits from exercise and movement. Those include:

- Increase of energy
- Release of endorphins, which give you an overall sense of feeling happy
- Helps you keep a healthy weight
- Improves your digestion
- Reduces inflammation
- Builds healthy bones

- Improves your sleep
- Helps you in maintaining a focused, sharper thinking and improves the memory
- Is beneficial to keep a good blood circulation

Walking barefoot in the fresh soil or in the sand, and swimming in the ocean is as well an excellent way to do some healthy movement and at the same time connect again with the electromagnetic conductivity of the Earth. Clint Ober et al. in the book, *Earthing* mention that just like the Earth, our bodies mostly contain water and minerals. Both are good conductors of electrons; the Earth is covered by electromagnetic layers, which is what creates the sensory response in our feet and in the paws of animals.

When you put your feet in the ground and get in touch with the soil, we draw electrical energy through our feet in the form of free electrons fluctuating at many frequencies. The direct conduct of electrons being conducted through our skin, regulate and destroy the free radicals in the body which are the main cause of inflammatory diseases. Ober et al. mention in the book that "These frequencies (provided by the Earth electrons) reset our biological clock and provide the body with electrical energy. The electrons themselves flow into the body, equalising it at the electrical potential to the Earth ( ) by reconnecting, you enable your body return to its normal electrical state, better able to self-regulate and self-heal".

ACTION:

Take your shoes off and go enjoy the free contact to the soil!

Take care of your mental garden

How are our thoughts originated?

The theory of reductionism in science, defines our thought process as a neuronal process which follows a certain pattern based on our views of the external environment. It is also acknowledged by science that those neuronal firing patterns are the effect of the bioelectrical function of our brain.

If we interact with certain frequencies that are of harm to our thought waves, the result can be translated into certain pattern of thoughts. Researchers in the topic of neuroscience concluded that the wavelengths from positive thoughts are different from the negative ones.

Behavioural scientist have also studied the effects on positive and negative thinking in regards to neuroplasticity[3] and they have found that optimist people are more likely to be successful in life and have a better physical health; Whereas the negative people tend to fall more easily in depressive states and have a more fragile physical health.

Dr Lou E. Whitaker, summarises the effects on the brain of positive and negative thinking derived from her research:

---

[3] Neuroplasticity: The ability of the brain to form and reorganise synaptic connections, especially in response to learning or experience or following injury (Oxford Dictionary)

Effects on the brain with positive thoughts:

- Improves ability to solve problems quicker and enhances creativity
- Improves ability to think faster and analyse data better
- Increases mental productivity by improving cognition
- Brain synapses (areas connecting neurons) increase dynamically
- Intensifies ability to pay attention and to focus

Effects of negative thoughts:

- Increased difficulty in processing thoughts and finding creative solutions
- Decreases activity in the cerebellum
- Decreases brain coordination
- Impacts the left temporal lobe (which is linked with fear mechanisms) which affects memory capacity, mood and impulse control

This is an interesting way to look at the effects that particular thoughts have in our psyche and our bodies. However, we are missing the primary answer to the very first question: Where do the thoughts really come from?

To think that our brain by itself generates the thoughts from the mind, reduces this world and our understanding of our existence as only 'material beings'. Since we do know that there are other 'worlds' in the metaphysical reality, I would like to introduce the idea of thoughts as 'collective energy forms'.

I relate with the idea that our 'thoughts' are not 'our own thoughts'. My mind, or my brain, do not generate by itself the 'thought'. I agree with Eckhart Tolle when he says that "human thoughts" are energy fields displayed in different vibrational frequencies. They originate in the 'collective human mind', and are basically flying in the air. Our mind, which is the software of the brain, 'picks up' a thought (an energy pattern) that resonates with that person at that specific moment. For example, let's say that I am driving my car and while on the highway, another car just changes to my lane without making any signalization.

As a result of this experience, if I am receptive of negativity, I feel angry and blame the driver of the other car. The human thought and sentiment of 'anger' possesses my mind for that moment in time, but is not 'my anger'. If on the other hand, I am more receptive for positivity, then my mind will pick a positive thought and thus I will feel more empathetic or simply see the experience and let it go, not letting any particular thought to 'possess' my mind.

I find the idea of the 'collective human thought' fascinating. If the thoughts we have are not really our thoughts but the result of a collective human mind, then all I have thought of 'myself' is not really me? If my brain would get transplanted to another body (if that would ever be possible) will the brain 'keep' the same mind or will it change because it has another body? And what will happen to the Self?

For the sake of practicality, we will not go so deep in the matter. This is a debate that has gone over millennia between the greatest scientists, philosophers, theologists, and other students of life and human behaviour. What is worthwhile mentioning here is that if our body and our thought process are not directly linked, then what we consider our mind, and more specifically our thoughts do not really represent our real Self.

Our Self operates beyond body and mind. Is an ever-present state of being. Transcends collective human thought, thus I do believe, our 'Selves' are the direct connection with the universe and with the divine.

The spark of uniqueness that gets a display through our 'Persona' by spontaneous action is a specific point of attention into the infinite.

To conclude this discussion, I personally believe that to take care of our mind is not only to keep it in a mentally positive state; but also to realise that the very nature of the Self is transcendental to everything we rationally 'know' and the only metaphysical measure is Love, which is directly connected to the present. Our thoughts are tools that our mind can use to detect if we are getting 'possessed' by Love or by lower states like Fear and Anger.

Take care of your spirit

"You must learn to get in touch with the innermost essence of your being. This true essence is beyond the ego. It is fearless; it is free; it is immune to criticism; it does not fear any challenge. It is beneath no one, superior to no one, and full of magic, mystery and enchantment."

- Deepak Chopra

One of the most fundamental truths in life, is the metaphysical aspect of our being. We are essentially not only our body and our mind; there is an intelligence well beyond our own comprehension that is orchestrating life on all its levels; including our own life. Some call it spirit, others energy, oneness, or God. I would like to recall at this point again the philosophy behind the existence of a spirit from the great philosophers like Kant and Schopenhauer which explain *Spirit* it as a phenomenon represented in this world as *the will to live* which transcends intellect because intellect comes mainly from the animal nature of our existence via the brain, whereas the *will to live* comes from the very source of life that we still lack to comprehend.

This will to live which contain in itself the source of divinity exists in all of us in metaphysical form. I like to call it spirit. Our spirit, which in reality is not of individual nature but fundamentally is a part of the totality of life, is what pulls us all together as a vital force. We tend to perceive our spirit as part of our own body and thinking, but like Schopenhauer says: "The world we perceive is characterized by great diversity, but this diversity is not fundamental; fundamentally the world is a unity".

People with great minds like Mahatma Gandhi, Maya Angelou, Martin Luther King, Steve Jobs, Nelson Mandela, among others, were known from placing their spirituality at the core of everything they did. Their strong faith in God which they also call it their inner voice or intuition, regardless of their religion, was manifested in their actions when they understood that the infinite intelligence operating through them is the closest they could get to grasp about what is the reality of themselves and their lives. The grandiosity of their actions, did not came from a narrow perspective about themselves; but more from an energy and intelligence far beyond even their own comprehension. Gandhi mentioned in his autobiography that for him, there was no better guidance in this world than his inner voice: "I had long taught myself to follow my inner voice. I delighted in submitting to it. To act against it would be painful and difficult for me".

To live a fully complete life as a human being, we cannot ignore our spirit. We have to listen to it, nourish it and put it at work, otherwise it stays dormant within us, like an old forgotten muscle. Your spirit talks to you every day, at every moment, even if you don't realise it. The problem is that we have been taught to suppress our own voice in favour of letting ourselves get overloaded with external opinions. We have learnt that the opinions of others about our personal lives have more value than our own. We let doctors judge our health, teachers judge our intelligence, bosses judge our capabilities and society judge our value based on their perception of what you produce or give. But in reality, no one but you know who you really are and what you can do.

Listening to your own inner voice, to your spirit, is a very powerful tool to stay connected to your true Self. I see your true Self as a unique expression of the whole universe. It's like if every person would represent a drop of water in the vast ocean: No drop is ever the same; each drop has its own individual expression, and even manifest itself in different material forms depending on the outside temperature: Some drops are represented on air as vapour; others as a rain drop; others as snow cups there are a million ways the water drops are manifested in the material world, but in essence, they come from the same source, from the same vast ocean.

The ocean would not exist without the drops, and the drops by themselves cannot exist without the ocean. Likewise, our own persona cannot exist without the spirit, and the spirit could not manifest its unique expression without taking material form through our bodies.

How to keep a strong connection with your Spirit

Pay attention to your emotions

One of the closest ways we have to detect the workings of our spirit is through our emotions. Our body already has built in the capability to alert us when something is right or wrong.

When navigating through life, we are constantly exposed to millions of situations. Every time we confront ourselves with a situation, it requires that we take a decision. It can be a tiny decision, like if you should wear the white or the green shoes; or big decisions, like who you will marry or which workplace you will join. When faced with such situations, our bodies always trigger certain feelings and emotions: We can feel excited, scared, mad, sad, happy, nervous, horrified, etc. You should always listen to your body and pay attention to the emotions you are experiencing, because most of the time is our spirit manifesting through the physical form giving us hints about what could be right or wrong for us in that particular case.

For example, let's imagine you are confronted with the difficult decision whether to divorce or to stay together with your partner. After listing all the logical reasons about what will happen if you stay together and what would happen if you split, what is what you are feeling at the core? Are you feeling sad, depressed and without willingness to keep going? Or do you feel beyond that, a sense of peace? A separation triggers of course a mix of emotions, but there is always one that dominates. You might feel for example sad and melancholic about leaving a life partner in the short term; but if you realise that most of the time when you were together you felt mainly miserable and hopeless, then in the great scheme of things, the separation might be the best decision, if it will bring more peace to both parties in the long term.

We should keep in mind that there are many layers of emotions; to identify the core emotion connected to your intuition will be hard work when you do not know yourself well. To identify the right emotion requires a profound knowledge of one's self. Most of the time, people confuse the first emotions they feel when they get exposed to a challenging situation, and think this is what their 'gut' tells them. It's normal to feel intense emotions when you are on the 'hot potato scene'. Therefore, is best to let time pass and let emotions 'calm down' to get a better perspective about the situation and from that place, it is much easier to identify the real emotion, delivered to you by your spirit.

Practice humility

Another way to connect more with your spirit is through practicing humility. That means, keeping away as much as possible from your Ego. How can you do that? It is for sure not an easy task. What helps is to first observe and recognise, which actions are more ego-driven, and which ones are more driven by love, or by a desire to help others.

Viktor Frankl, author of the famous book, *Man in Search of a Meaning*, calls this practice the self-transcendence of existence, which he describes, it's an essential capacity a man must develop if he or she aims to find meaning. It implies that a person should always direct his or her life efforts in order to benefit someone else, beyond the own self; let it be in favour of a cause, or a person. The more you forget about yourself and throw yourself to the cause or person you love, the more human you become and the more your brain and body capacities get perfectioned. So, we can say that humility - which is forgetting about ourselves and dedicating our cause to the benefit of others - brings automatically a higher connection to our spirit, which is the one that will take the lead and operate through our actions.

Stay connected to your heart

I believe the spirit's main physical connection to the body is the heart, the place in our body where our spirit manifests. Our heart is really the key inner messenger that whispers to us what is important for us and helps in finding our life purpose. It even helps us in finding out how we should get there. If you follow your heart more than your intellect, you will be sure to be following always the right path.

For some of us, it can be very challenging to recognise what comes from the heart and what from the intellect. But if you pay close attention, you will discover that your body is the wisest counsellor. Sometimes it just helps to pay attention to your emotions and feelings, like I mentioned previously. Some people say for example, *"When my gut tells me something is not good, I start to feel a pain, a sort of pressure in my stomach"*. Or *"If I have strong heart beats and I start to get anxious, I know I am in front of a situation that will be life-changing for me"*. When something excites us in a positive way, we might feel nervous, have strong heartbeats, but also feel a lot of excitement. Those feelings and emotions combined are telling you that this is something big, important, that should be followed. Or on the contrary, if you are about to take a decision that makes you feel anxious, you feel a pressure in the chest, an overall feeling of uneasiness, even a bit depressed, then your body is telling you that maybe this is not the right direction.

A word of caution: our heart does not necessarily guide us towards what feels pleasurable to avoid pain. Our heart 'feeling' goes beyond the sensations of pleasure and pain and operates in the metaphysical, beyond our physical senses. That's why what is pleasurable, and gives you a sensation of happiness in the short term does not necessarily mean that is a signal from the spirit that this is correct; the same applies to pain: Not everything that is painful in the short term and triggers sensations of uneasiness or fear means that the spirit is telling you not to do something. We need to learn to differentiate a feel-good, immediate sensation and relief of pain versus a higher dimension, a higher sense of feeling congruent, complete and joyful, by following what you love regardless of the challenges you will encounter to reach the desirable outcome.

Your spiritual self is the life-energy manifesting through you in many different ways: giving you life-energy forces that enables you to use your body, allowing your mind and intellect to provide and guide the directions for your body, and as act as an inner compass, whose magnet drags you to the desired direction.

When I went to South Africa and visited the loggerhead sea turtle's reserve in Cape Town, I learned an amazing fact. Turtles are born with an internal compass, which helps them to know where they are at any moment and also guides them in the right migratory route so they can get enough feeding and also know where they can swim off to hide their eggs, depending on the seasons, and they do it with hundred percent precision. They don't need any technological gadget like a GPS. They just instinctively do it.

How they do it is still a mystery, although researchers believe turtles can detect latitudes and follow the magnetic fields of the Earth. But even if they are born with that quality, how can they *know* there is enough warm, enough food and a safe place for their eggs, without being there yet?

I believe we have the same internal compass in ourselves. All we need to do is let nature do her job and let ourselves be guided. Let the intellect do its work in the 'physical realm' but also let space in the present for the intuition do his magic. Are you longing to reach your North Star? Listen to your spirit! I'm sure it *knows*.

To close this section, I would like to leave you with this thought: To be successful, you have to incessantly and courageously work in developing the powerful synergy of body, mind and spirit working together towards your North Star. Life is for sure not easy, but if you manage to maintain the powerful synergy together, there is nothing in this life that will stop you from reaching your craziest dreams!

#TheKnechtWay to maintain a powerful synergy body-mind-spirit

To reach high levels of success, you need to have a lot of energy; that means a strong healthy body, a sharp mind and a well-nourished spirit:

- Our body, in its physical form, is a biochemical, bioelectrical organisms that interacts with the immediate environment all the time; everything around us has a direct effect in our health;

- To keep the body functioning at an optimal level, you need to eat high-quality foods: fresh foods, raw vegetables and grains;

- Follow the alkaline diet: eighty percent alkaline foods, twenty percent acidic;

- Seek for professional help if you are unsure about what kind of diet is best for you

- Drink water when you are thirsty; do not overload it with water as it slows metabolism;

- Movement is life. Maintain a healthy sports schedule; a thirty-minute walk daily is an excellent start;

- Your mental garden is as important as the physical one. Keep your mind healthy with positive and inspiring thoughts and suppress the negative ones as much as possible;

- Your spirit is ultimately what keeps your whole machinery alive. Connect with the divine source; listen to your emotions, find your internal compass;

- Find your own wisdom. The source is there ready to be used. Go inside and grab it!

BONUS:

Go to the Success Mindset website and download the free booklet to get a list of recommended books, articles and videos about this exciting topic of keeping the body-mind-spirit balance.

Questions for Reflection

1. What is your personal commitment to increase your energy levels?

2. Throughout this section, we went through different ways you can get a closer connection with your spirit. Which one resonated with you the most? Can you think about other ways to connect to your spirit?

3. Which activities can help you to get an optimal connection to the triada: body-mind-soul?

Observe which activities in your daily life you can delegate to your inner wisdom. What comes to your mind?

Final words

Success, in the highest of forms, is a way to find the meaning of your life. It's something that is first created and envisioned from the inside. What you believe you are is what you end up becoming. The definition of success is a very personal definition. No one can tell you how success looks for you. You can choose. You can choose to follow the mainstream, one size fits all, and work your ass off trying to please others, or you can choose to define and live your own success, at your own rhythm and with your own terms.

Remember that you have the power to control your own destiny. You are the captain of your soul. There will never be someone like you, ever. It is your responsibility and duty, to make the best out of your existence. Start now, right where you are, with what you have. It's never too late to take the mast of your boat and start sailing towards the dreamland, the land where you will finally find the best version of yourself!

To access the free booklet to support your reading journey, visit the Success Mindset webpage:

https://paolaknecht.lpages.co/the-success-mindset/

I sincerely hope that you have enjoyed this journey of self-discovery. There is nothing I love more than to be a little part of it. If that is the case and this book has been a help for you, I would love to hear about it! Write me a note on my social media using the hashtag #SuccessWithKnecht.

Also, if you believe this book could help someone else, do not hesitate to pass the voice!

Now put your shoes on, and enjoy the run!

Acknowledgements

Ideas come to you in the most unexpected ways. I was in the hospital bed recovering from the birth of my second son, Henry back in late March 2020 when the first idea of writing this book came to my mind.

I understood my life was about to have a three hundred and sixty-degree change again. Being a mother of a newborn and a three-year-old girl, I was going to spend many months away from the coaching practice and from personal contact, which made me wonder: How can I stay close to people and help them, even if is not physically possible?

And that's when the book was born. My hope is to continue helping people in ways that overcome the barriers of time and physical contact.

This book wouldn't have been possible without the unconditional support of my husband Marc and my lovely children Salma and Henry. I want to thank them from the bottom of my heart for being in my life and for being my greatest motivation.

Special thanks as well to my editor, Kirsten Rees and her team who did a wonderful job in bringing this book to life. As well as David Colon for designing a fantastic book cover.

I'm very grateful to all my coaching clients who were my source of inspiration and the reason why I wrote this book. A big thank you to my wonderful clients Lisa, Andrea and Mirka who let me share their success stories. To my beta readers and fellow writers who took the time to give me an honest review and challenged me to bring my ideas to the next level.

I'm also extremely grateful to my lifelong friends Laura, Isabel, Denise, Roxana, Gloria and Claudia who have been with me in key moments of my life and were of course there as a supporting nest while

I was writing this book. To my mentors, specially Jordan, Raimón and Manuela, who also inspired and encouraged me to compile all the learnings from all these years of research and discovery and share them with you through this book.

Last but not least my mom, Martha. She was the first person that believed in me unconditionally and always supported my crazy ideas. I love you Mommy. Thank you for believing in me.

Finally, as Carl Sagan once said: "Books are proof that humans can do magic". I am eternally grateful to be able to learn from wonderful people, leaders of all sorts and from all walks of life, who cared enough to write their legacies so that we all can learn from them. They certainly made the path clearer and stronger for generations to come.

ABOUT THE AUTHOR

 Paola Knecht is a leadership & transformational coach, and author.

The founder of My Mindpower Coaching & Consulting, Paola is dedicated to helping people improve all areas of their lives.

After working more than fifteen years in global renowned companies, she decided to give a complete shift to her life and do what she really cares about: to become an author and help people all around the world to find their personal life's meaning through coaching.

She lives in Switzerland with her husband and two children.

If you wish to discover more about Paola's coaching services, visit:

www.my-mindpower.com

Or send a direct email to paola.knecht@my-mindpower.com

To follow for upcoming publications, visit her author webpage:

https://www.amazon.com/author/paolaknecht

To access the free booklet to support your reading journey, visit the Success Mindset webpage:

https://paolaknecht.lpages.co/the-success-mindset/

I would love to know what you think of *The Success Mindset.* You can write a review at the following below or write me a personal note at paola.knecht@my-mindpower.com.

- Amazon - https://www.amazon.com/author/paolaknecht
- Facebook - Search Paola Knecht
- Goodreads - Search Paola Knecht

To follow Paola:

Instagram: @paolaknecht_author

Twitter @PaolaKnecht

LinkedIn: https://www.linkedin.com/in/paolaknecht/

Appendix I

Here is a list of universal values that you can use as guidance for the exercise *Find your Core Values* suggested in the Second Pillar of Success.

You can also download a free template for the exercise in the downloadable booklet available on the Success Mindset website.

Competence	Pleasure	Leadership
Change	Positivity	Independence
Simplicity	Decisiveness	Adventure
Luxury	Commitment	Self-respect
Tradition	Reputation	Maturity
Elegance	Justice	Openness
Travel	Human Rights	Leisure
Outdoors	Diversity	Joy
Love	Religion	Punctuality
Romance	Spirituality	Order
Family	Loyalty	Discipline
Cooperation	Excellence	Stability
Responsiveness	Quality	Accuracy
Service	Charitable	Democracy

Recognition	Accountability	World Peace
Community	Authenticity	Equality
Unity	Freedom	Diversity
Passion	Solitude	Harmony
Education	Inspiration	Cooperation
Wisdom	Faith	Meaningful
Truth	Comfort	Empowerment
Inner Peace	Health	Competition
Solving- Problems	Ambition	Ethics
Security	Sexuality	Wealth
Prosperity	Creativity	Fairness
Power	Arts	Community
Stability	Culture	Locality
	Beauty	Globalization

Appendix II:

Main Sources

Allen, James. *As a Man Thinketh*. Connecticut: Martino Fine Books, 2018 (reprinted edition from 1918)

Al Maktoum, Mohamed Bin Rashid. *Reflections about Happiness and Positivity*. Dubai, UAE: Explorer Publishing and Distribution, 2017

Bettger, Frank. *How I Raised Myself From Failure To Success In Selling*. Touchstone. Kindle Edition, 1992

Beckwith, Michael Bernard (2021): *Home*. https://michaelbeckwith.com/

Blume, Judy (2021): *About Judy*. https://judyblume.com/about-judy-blume/

Biography (8 February 2021): *Tom Brady*. https://www.biography.com/athlete/tom-brady

Brown, Brené. *Dare to Lead*. Ebury Publishing. Kindle Edition, 2018

Brown, Brené. *Daring Greatly*. Penguin Books Ltd. Kindle Edition, 2016

Canfield, Jack, Switzer Janet. *The Success Principles*. Toronto: HarperCollins Publisher, 2015

Collins, Jim. *From Good to Great*. Harper Business Publishing, 2001

Cook, Colin; Wind, Yoram (Jerry), Gunther, Robert. *The Power of Impossible Thinking*, Pearson Education. Kindle Edition.

Coyle, Daniel. *El Pequeño Libro del Talento (Spanish Edition)*. Penguin Random House Grupo Editorial España. Kindle Edition.

Chopra, Deepak; Snyder, Kimberly. *Radical Beauty*. Ebury Publishing. Kindle Edition.

Chopra, Deepak. *The Seven Spiritual Laws of Success: A Practical Guide to the Fulfillment of Your Dreams*. Amber-Allen Publishing. Kindle Edition

D'Antonio Michael. Never Enough: *Donald Trump and the Pursuit of Success*. New York: Macmillan USA, 2015

E. Puterman, J. Lin, E. Blackburn, et al., *"The Power of Exercise: Buffering the Effect of Chronic Stress on Telomere Length,"* PLoS One 5, no. 5 (May 2010): e10837, doi:10.1371/journal.pone.0010837.

Eger, Edith. *La Bailarina de Auschwitz*. Spanish Edition. Barcelona: Editorial Planeta, 2018

Fast Company (25 February 2015*): Personal Mission Statements Of 5 Famous CEOs (And Why You Should Write One Too).*

https://www.fastcompany.com/3026791/personal-mission-statements-of-5-famous-ceos-and-why-you-should-write-one-too

Frankl, Viktor. *El hombre en Busca de Sentido (Spanish Edition)*. Herder Editorial. Kindle

Edition, 2015

Franklin, Benjamin. *The Autobiography of Benjamin Franklin: Illustrated*. Kindle edition.

Greene, Robert. *The Laws of Human Nature*. London: Penguin Random House, 2018

Goggins, David. *Can't Hurt Me: Master Your Mind and Defy the Odds*. Lioncrest Publishing. Kindle Edition.

Hardy, Darren: *The Compound Effect*. New York: Vanguard Press, 2012

Harris, Elizabeth (31 August 2020): *Trump Books Keep Coming, And Readers Can't Stop Buying*. https://www.ny-times.com/2020/08/31/books/trump-books.html

Harari, Yuval Noah. *Sapiens: A Brief History of Human Kind*. Canada: Penguin Random House, 2014

Issacson, Walter. *Steve Jobs*. New York: Simon & Schuster Paperbacks, 2011

Jenny, Hans. *Cymatics: A study of Wave Phenomena & Vibration*. English Edition. Macromedia Publishing, 2001

Johnson, Paul. *Socrates*. Penguin Publishing Group. Kindle Edition

Kafka, Franz. *The Metamorphosis*. CreateSpace Independent Publishing Platform, 1915

Kishimi Ichiro, Koga Fumitake. *The Courage to be Disliked*. London: Atria Books, 2018

Kubala, Jillian (3 September 2020): *6 Acidic Foods - Should you avoid them?*

https://www.healthline.com/nutrition/acidic-foods#recommendation

Lester, Dawn; Parker, David. *What Really Makes You Ill?: Why Everything You Thought You Knew About Disease Is Wrong*. Kindle Edition.

Mandela, Nelson. *Un Largo Camino hacia la Libertad (A Long Walk to Freedom)*. Spanish Edition. Translated by Antonio Resines and Herminia Bevia. Barcelona: Penguin Random House Group, 2016

Masaru, Emoto. *The Hidden Messages in Water*. English Edition. New York: Atria Books, 2005

Maltz, Maxwell. *Psycho-Cybernetics*. Deluxe Edition. Penguin Publishing Group. Kindle Edition, 2015

Marcial Pérez, David (7 December 2020): *López Obrador nombra a Tatiana Clouthier como nueva secretaria de economía.*

https://elpais.com/mexico/2020-12-07/lopez-obrador-nombra-a-tatiana-clouthier-como-nueva-secretaria-de-economia.html

M.K. Gandhi. *An Autobiography or The Story of My Experiments with Truth*. Navajivan Trust. Kindle Edition

Murray, Scott (17 February 2017): *Gary Payer: "I became a champion because I know how it was to suffer."*

https://www.theguardian.com/sport/2017/jul/17/small-talk-gary-player-open-golf

Murphy, Bill (January 23, 2021). *12 Key Secrets of Tom Brady's Success, Quickly Explained and Then Ranked by How Easy They Are to Copy.*

https://www.inc.com/bill-murphy-jr/12-key-secrets-of-tom-bradys-success-quickly-explained-then-ranked-by-how-easy-they-are-to-copy.html

Murphy, Mark (15 April 2018): *Neuroscience Explains Why You Need To Write Down Your Goals If You Actually Want To Achieve Them.*

https://www.forbes.com/sites/markmurphy/2018/04/15/neuro-science-explains-why-you-need-to-write-down-your-goals-if-you-actually-want-to-achieve-them/

National Geographic (10 October 2010). *¿En qué consiste el miedo?*

https://www.nationalgeographic.es/ciencia/en-que-consiste-el-miedo

Ober, Clinton; Sinatra, Stephen T; Zucker, Martin. *Earthing*. Turner Publishing Company. Kindle Edition.

Office of Disease Prevention, Health and Promotion (22 February 2016): *2008 Physical Activity Guidelines for Americans: Summary*

http://health.gov/paguidelines/guidelines/summary.aspx.

Oxford Dictionary (2021): Definition of Passion.

https://www.oxfordlearnersdictionaries.com/definition/english/passion

Oxford Dictionary (2021): Definition of Fear.

https://www.oxfordlearnersdictionaries.com/definition/american_english/fear_1

Oxford Dictionary (2021): Definition of Resilience.

https://www.oxfordlearnersdictionaries.com/definition/english/resilience

Oxford Dictionary (2021): Definition of Pressure.

https://www.oxfordlearnersdictionaries.com/definition/english/pressure_1?q=Pressure

Peterson, Jordan B. *12 Rules for Life*. Random House of Canada. Kindle Edition, 2018

Popper, Karl; Eccles John. *The Self and Its Brain*. Berlin: Springer-Verlag, 1977

Rao, Joe (16 May 2017): *The North Star: Polaris*.

https://www.space.com/15567-north-star-polaris.html

Robbins, Tony. *Controle Su Destino*. Spanish Edition. Translated by: José Manuel Pomares. Barcelona: Penguin Random House, 1992

Sadhguru. *Inner Engineering*. Random House Publishing Group. Kindle Edition.

Schwalfenberg, Gary (12 October 2012): *The Alkaline Diet: Is there evidence that an Alkaline pH Diet Benefits Health?*

https://www.ncbi.nlm.nih.gov/pmc/articles/PMC3195546/

Schopenhauer, Arthur; Books, Manor. *Essays of Schopenhauer*. AB Books. Kindle Edition.

Science News (8 August 2014): *How we form habits and change existing ones*. https://www.sciencedaily.com/releases/2014/08/140808111931.htm

Shiva, Vandana. *Staying Alive: Women, Ecology and Development*. California: North Atlantic Books, 2010

The Human Memory (25 November 2020): *Memory Encoding*. https://human-memory.net/memory-encoding/

The Best Brain Possible (5 August 2018): *The Neuroscience of Building a Resilient Brain*. https://thebestbrainpossible.com/neuroscience-resilient-brain-stress/#:~:text=Resilience%20is%20not%20a%20trait,and%20it%20can%20be%20learned

Tolle, Eckhart. *The Power of Now: A Guide to Spiritual Enlightenment*. Spanish Edition. Translated by Miguel Iribarren. Vancouver: Namaste Publishing Inc., 1997

Trump, Donald J.; Zanker, Bill. *Think Big*. HarperCollins e-books. Kindle Edition, 2007

Trump, Donald. *The Art of the Deal*. Random House. Kindle Edition, 2016

V. Lobo, A. Patil, A. Phatak, et al., *"Free Radicals, Antioxidants and Functional Foods: Impact on Human Health,"* Pharmacognosy Reviews 4, no. 8 (2010): 118–26, doi:10.4103/0973-7847.70902.Wang, Kaitlyn (June 21, 2017): *Jack Ma's top 5 Tips for Long Term Success*.

https://www.inc.com/kaitlyn-wang/jack-ma-alibaba-tips-for-success.html

Watts, Allan. *The Book On The Taboo Against Knowing Who You Are*. London: Souvenir Press, 2009

Whitaker, Lou Ed. D (2017): *How Does Thinking Positive Thought Affects Neuroplasticity?*
https://meteoreducation.com/how-does-thinking-positive-thoughts-affect-neuroplasticity/
Williams, Serena (2021): *Serena's World.*

https://www.serenawilliams.com/pages/bio

Winfrey, Oprah. *What I know for Sure*. UK: Macmillan Publishers Limited, 2014

Made in United States
North Haven, CT
16 November 2021